I Burned at the Feast

I Burned at the Feast
Selected Poems of Arseny Tarkovsky

translated by
Philip Metres and Dimitri Psurtsev

Cleveland State University Poetry Center
Cleveland, Ohio

ISBN 978-0-9963167-0-5

First edition

19 18 17 16 15   5 4 3 2 1

This book is published by the Cleveland State University Poetry Center,
2121 Euclid Avenue, Cleveland, Ohio 44115-2214
www.csupoetrycenter.com and is distributed by
SPD / Small Press Distribution, Inc. www.spdbooks.org.

Cover image: Frame from "Mirror" (1974), a film by Andrey Tarkovsky.
    Reproduced with permission from Mosfilm Cinema Concern.
I Burned at the Feast was designed and typeset by Amy Freels in Palatino.

LIBRARY OF CONGRESS CATALOGING-IN-PUBLICATION DATA
Tarkovsky, Arseny, 1907–1989
    [Poems. Selections. English]
    I burned at the feast : selected poems of Arseny Tarkovsky / translated by Philip
Metres and Dimitri Psurtsev. — First edition.
        pages cm
    Includes bibliographical references.
    ISBN 978-0-9963167-0-5
    I. Metres, Philip, 1970- translator. II. Psurtsev, Dimitri, translator. III. Title.

PG3489.A67A2 2015
891.71'44—dc23

                        2015003981

Acknowledgments

Grateful acknowledgment is due to the following journals for publishing versions of these poems:

Artful Dodge: "Field Hospital"

Asymptote: "Cricket," "My sight, which was my power, now blurs," "Valya's Willow"

Atlanta Review: "The Word"

Circumference: "Hail on First Petit-Bourgeois Street," "The Hunt," "The Poet," "Olives," and "Reality and Speech"

Congeries: "Candle," "Portrait," "Don't Stand Here"

Cosmonauts Avenue: "Once Upon a Time"

Diode: "The gun battery was over there, behind that hill," "Here, a house once stood. Inside, some old man," "And now summer has left," "I bid farewell to everything I was," "Steppe"

The Freeman: "Life, Life," "The Night Before the First of June"

Guernica: "Song Under the Bullet," "A German machinegunner will shoot me in the road, or"

Gulf Coast: "Afterword: Erotic Soyuz," "Butterfly in the Hospital Orchard"

The Journal: "O, if only I could rise, regain memory and consciousness"

jubilat: "By the book of stone I learn a tongue outside of time," "The Sugakleya disappears into the reeds"

Knot: "Wind," "From its dark sleep the body wakes," "That thunder still rings in the ears," "Wet-nurse of dragonflies and birds," "Snow in March"

Massachusetts Review: "Refugee"

Mead: the Magazine of Literature and Libations: "Infant-Life," "Pigeons," "Eurydice"

Michigan Quarterly Review: "Western Sky," "Things"
Modern Poetry in Translation (UK): "My sight, which was my
    power, now blurs"
New England Review: "Saturday, June 21st, 1941,"
    "Ignatievo Forest," "Beautiful Day"
North American Review: "Manuscript"
PEN website: five poems from "Chistopol Notebook"
Poetry: "To Poems," "A blind man was riding an unheated train"
St. Petersburg Review: "The table is set for six," "I've come to hate
    them, these words, words, words," "Yesterday morning I
    began waiting for you," "Van Gogh"
Transference: "After the War"
Two Lines: "The Book of Grass," "You evening light, gray"
Two Lines online: "I learned the grass as I began to write"
Voltage: "First Times Together"
Waxwing: "If I were the arrogant man I once was," "Poets," "Passing
    By," "Their commas exact and sensible," "To the Memory
    of A .A. Akhmatova"

Thanks to Marina Arsenyevna Tarkovskaya, for keeping alive the
memory of her father and his poetry, which continues to inspire gen-
erations of readers.

Published with the support of the Institute for Literary Translation
(Russia). Translation of this publication and the creation of its layout
were carried out with the financial support of the Federal Agency for
Press and Mass Communication under the federal target program
"Culture of Russia (2012–2018)."

Thanks to the Mikhail Prokhorov Fund (Russia) for their generous
support in bringing this project to publication. Thanks as well to John
Carroll University, the Thomas J. Watson Foundation, the National
Endowment for the Arts (for an Individual Artist Grant), to the Ohio
Arts Council (for an Individual Excellence Grant), the PEN/Heim
Translation Fund, and the Creative Workforce Fellowship. The Creative
Workforce Fellowship is a program of the Community Partnership for
Arts and Culture. The Fellowship program is supported by the resi-
dents of Cuyahoga County through a public grant from Cuyahoga Arts
& Culture.

Thanks to Michele Berdy, Daniel Bourne, Amy Breau, Camille Dungy, Olga Isayeva, Ilya Kaminsky, E.J. McAdams, Don Share, Tatiana Tulchinsky, and Christian Wiman, for their editorial suggestions and encouragement.

Over twenty years ago, the first seeds of this book were planted in the Den of the Voice. Thanks to our families for enduring five full years of poem-drafts, late night interrogations, and endless email consultations.

And finally, to the Cleveland State University Poetry Center, Director Caryl Pagel, and to former Interim Director Frank Giampietro—for their belief in this book, meticulous editing, and helping to bring it to life.

Contents

II. The Earthly Feast (1945–1965)

Introduction

Arseny Alexandrovich Tarkovsky was born in the Ukrainian city of Elisavetgrad (now Kirovohrad) in 1907 and moved to Moscow in 1923, working as a newspaper journalist and publishing his first poems. By the late 1930s, he had become a noted translator of Turkmen, Georgian, Armenian, Arabic, and other Asian poets. During the Second World War, he served as a war correspondent for the Soviet Army publication *Battle Alarm* from 1942 to 1944, receiving the Order of the Red Star for valor. He would come to write some of the most stunning and intimate poems about the Second World War, which, unlike many popular war poems of the time, viewed war through an unheroic lens. His first book of poems had been accepted for publication in 1946, but in the wake of Andrei Zhdanov's ideological attack on the celebrated writers Anna Akhmatova and Mikhail Zoshchenko, the book was never published. Tarkovsky's first volume of his own poems, *Before the Snow*, finally emerged in 1962, when the poet was 55, and rapidly sold out. His fame widened when his son, the internationally-acclaimed filmmaker Andrei Tarkovsky, included some of his father's poems in his films. He died in 1989, just before the Soviet Union fell.

In an interview toward the end of her life, Akhmatova called Arseny Tarkovsky the one "real poet" in the Soviet Union. In her words, "of all contemporary poets Tarkovsky alone is completely his own self, completely independent. He possesses the most important feature of a poet, which I'd call the birthright." Twenty-five years later, in 1992, in an introduction to the complete works of Tarkovsky in Russian, critic Yuri Kublanovsky effused that:

Tarkovsky managed to keep his creative mind undamaged and free. What I mean, of course, is not just freedom from propaganda, but also the principal freedom, inner freedom, the one defined by [Alexander] Blok as the secret freedom of humanity. Somehow he never succumbed to the temptation of pleasing—not only the criminal authorities, but also to a more subtle temptation of pleasing the reading public—of tuning, half-consciously, while writing, to their demands.

In his poetic and spiritual freedom, Tarkovsky outlasted the slag and dross of totalitarianism. His poetry is the internal cinema of the Soviet era, an unscrolling testimony of the gentle ferocity of a soul surviving a deadly and soul-crushing period.

The last of the great twentieth century Russian poets, and still virtually unknown in the West, Tarkovsky emerged as the youngest force of the Silver Age poets he'd read (and often knew personally)—including Osip Mandelstam, Marina Tsvetaeva, and Anna Akhmatova. Paradoxically, he did this by creating a bridge back to the Golden Age of Russian poetry during this bleak period. At the time, official Russian poetry was anything but independent, and the great poets had gone silent or underground under the rule of Stalin and Socialist Realism. Mandelstam had asked, famously:

My age, my beast, who could
Look into your eyes
And glue with blood
The vertebrae of two centuries?

After Mandelstam died, Tarkovsky carried on the great poet's poetic and cultural surgery.

Yet Tarkovsky's poems were more than an extension of Mandelstam's project. Vivid in its stunning musicality, teeming with Biblical allusions, Tarkovsky's verse maintained its resolute allegiance to a poetic tradition that hearkened back to the origins of Russian poetry. Tarkovsky drew from the sound and vision of Alexander Pushkin—Russia's Shakespeare—whose intoxicatingly primordial music transformed Russian poetry a century before. Tarkovsky's poems exude a poignant gratitude, marked by a childlike wonder for nature, though they are set against the backdrop of heartbreak during one of the most tragic periods of Russian history.

This comprehensive bilingual edition of selected poems— the first of its kind—gathers Arseny Tarkovsky's astonishing verse, balancing between representing the canonical view of Tarkovsky's finest work in Russian and choosing our most felicitiously translated versions in English. Structured in roughly chronological order, the book's three main sections correspond to cataclysmic historical and poetical change: "Butterfly in the Hospital Orchard," "The Earthly Feast," and "Gather My Wax When Morning Arrives." Together, these poems tell the story of a poet who, despite terrible losses, endured, and came to produce a uniquely mystical vision.

"Butterfly in the Hospital Orchard" preserves some of Tarkovsky's most accomplished early verse, often about the angst of love and loss, and segues into his stunning poems set during the Second World War.

Though his poetry of the 1920s and 1930s was sometimes considered imitative of Mandelstam, even the early poems demonstrate Tarkovsky's characteristic hauntedness, a departure from Mandelstam's Acmeistic clarity. Consider "Candle"— how even in youth, the poet saw the evanescence of mortal life:

A small yellow tongue flickers.
The candle drips and drips.
This is how you and I live—
our souls flare, flesh disappears.

In "The table is set for six," Tarkovsky creates a spectral gathering, a scene from the past brought into the grief-ridden present, in which he spends an evening around the table with his long-dead family—his father Alexander Karlovich, his brother Valya, and his first love Maria Faltz, who had died of tuberculosis eight years earlier, in 1932:

From the dark, the wine sings
and the crystal rings:
How much we loved you,
How many winters ago.

My father would smile at me,
my brother, pour some wine.
Her ringless hand in mine,
the woman would say:

My heels are caked with dirt,
my plaited hair's gone clear,
and our voices now call out
from under the earth.

In the poem's conditional tense, everything is happening as
it happened, but differently. As if the film of memory plays out
across a screen, but the projector has caught fire, and the woman
he loved is visible but is now being consumed by the flames.

If his love poems are haunted, Tarkovsky's war poems con-
tain moments of sardonic humor (see, in particular, "Don't
stand here" and "A German machinegunner will shoot me in
the road, or"); unforgettable beauty; and longing and delight. In
poems like "Western Sky," Tarkovsky places war's devastation
alongside the orienting and healing beauty of the natural world:

On patches of unreaped rye
boats of gold descend.
How close you come, evening sky,
to my scorched steppe.

Your sails so pink and delicate.
Chart a new course
from trenches and bomb craters,
draw us to your gentle waters.

Since the poem addresses the "sky"—in Russian, the word
"небо" could mean both sky and heaven—Tarkovsky's poem is
also a quiet, awe-filled prayer.

In other war poems, such as "Here, a house once stood. Inside, some old man" Tarkovsky's attention to the excruciating details of a destroyed home alternates dizzyingly between resignation and traumatic clarity:

> Here, a house once stood. Inside, some old man
> lived with a child. And now the house is gone.
>
> A hundred kilo bomb — the earth, blacker than black.
> A home, now none. That's war; what can be done?
>
> On a heap of gray rags, a samovar gleams.
> A dresser, nearby a horse. Above the horse, steam.

Tarkovsky's juxtapositions—gray rags and samovar, dresser and horse, horse and steam—devastate and vex. We don't know whether the horse is alive and the steam rises above his warm body, or the horse is recently dead and the steam is the last vestige of his living warmth. That in Russian, *samovar* (an image of human warmth and tea-making) rhymes with the horse's steam makes the poem uncanny. Tarkovsky's poem invites the question: why, during wartime, should horses steam and samovars sit heaped among rags?

The war also lays Tarkovsky bare to primal vulnerability and our human longing to survive. His poem "Butterfly in the Hospital Orchard" is at once an ode to a butterfly, as the poet straddles the border between life and death, and a prayer that his soul does not depart from his body:

> Don't fly off to the East, O
> my lady! Don't chase the East,
> flying from shadows
> into the light. My soul, why
> do you long for a far-off place?

Tarkovsky's poetic cycle "Chistopol Notebook" (1941) deserves particular mention for its melding of personal and national grief. Against the backdrop of the invasion of the Soviet Union, when Russian losses were mounting and the prospects of a quick victory had faded, Tarkovsky was confronting his own personal tragedy. Written in Chistopol, an administrative center in Tartarstan where the Soviet Union of Writers evacuated from Moscow during the Nazi bombing campaign, Tarkovsky lays bare his grief and guilt over the suicide of the legendary poet, Marina Tsvetaeva, who had recently returned to the Soviet Union after seventeen years of exile and had become Tarkovsky's friend.

Tarkovsky had received a letter of praise from Tsvetaeva in October 1940, after the publication of a book of his translations of the Turkmen poet Mämmetweli Kemine. Tsvetaeva wrote: "your translation is charming. What can you do yourself? Because for another, you can do—everything. Find (and love)—and the words will be yours." In the same letter, she had invited him to her apartment to hear her recite her poems, and their friendship developed. However, Tsvetaeva, at forty-eight and nearly ten years his senior, had wanted more than friendship, and Tarkovsky had chosen not to become romantically involved.

Shortly after her return to Russia, Tsvetaeva, lacking the privileges of those in the Writers Union, had evacuated to nearby Yelabuga, Tartarstan in 1941. Unable to find work there, she moved again to Chistopol in August, where she found work as a dishwasher. After the arrest of her husband and daughter, and without means to provide for herself and her son George, she hanged herself on August 31, 1941. In a note to her son, she wrote:

> Forgive me, but to go on would be worse. I am gravely ill, this is not me anymore. I love you passionately. Do understand that I could not live anymore. Tell Papa and Alya, if you ever see them, that I loved them to the last moment and explain to them that I found myself in a trap.

Tarkovsky's grief was fierce. Compounding that grief, he came to learn that her final poem, dated March 1941—employing the first line of "The table is set for six" as an epigraph—was an aggrieved riposte to Tarkovsky's rejection to Tsvetaeva's amorousness.

Tarkovsky's "Chistopol Notebook" captures a poet struggling with his failure to help Tsvetaeva. In the face of a seemingly-doomed military conflict, and the tragedy of the suicide of a brilliant and tormented friend and his part in it, Tarkovsky keens his helplessness:

> I call, but Marina does not reply. She sleeps today
> so soundly in Yelabuga. Yelabuga, cemetery clay,
>
> You should be called a god-forgotten bog.
> At your name, like a bolt, the gates should be locked.
>
> Yelabuga, you'd have no trouble scaring orphans.
> Swindlers and robbers should lie in your coffins.
>
> On whom did you breathe your fierce frost,
> becoming her final earthly rest?
>
> Whose swan's cry did you hear before dawn?
> Tsvetaeva's. You heard Marina's last word.
>
> I'm freezing in your cemetery wind.
> Cursed, spruce-stabbed Yelabuga, give back Marina.

Reeling from these losses, working as a war correspondent at the front, Tarkovsky faced a second tragedy. In 1943, while stationed at the Soviet front near Vitebsk, Tarkovsky was shot in the leg. As a result of the percussion bullet wound, Tarkovsky contracted gaseous gangrene, and would undergo six progressive amputations in what was finally a failed attempt to salvage the leg.

Over a decade later, Tarkovsky's ordeal becomes the basis for a new vision in "Field Hospital":

> My lips were covered with sores, and also
> I was fed by a spoon, and also

I could not remember my name,
but the language of King David came
alive on my tongue.

In the poems that comprise the section "The Earthly Feast,"
Tarkovsky expands his poetic palette, moving from the dark
interiors of strikingly personal poetry toward a broader cosmic
vision. Though this period of his writing has been considered
transitional by some Russian critics—a form of post-war, post-
amputation silence—we can see glimmers of his mystical poet-
ics. In "I learned the grass as I began to write," Tarkovsky
professes this cosmic vision of the poet as a New Adam, and the
world a potential Eden:

I learned the grass as I began to write,
and the grass started whistling like a flute.
I gathered how color and sound could join
and when the dragonfly whirred up his hymn—
passing through green frets like a comet—
I knew a tear in each drop of dew.
Knew that in each facet of the huge eye,
in each rainbow of brightly churring wings,
dwells the burning word of the prophet—
by some miracle I found Adam's secret.

Critic Sergei Chuprinin has written that Tarkovsky's gift was
seeing "heaven in a wildflower," alluding to Blake's poem. Tar-
kovsky's interest in mysticism, rare among Russian poets dur-
ing the enforced atheism of the Soviet age, explored both a
transcendental Judeo-Christian vision of humanity and an
immanent pantheism. In a poem such as "Earthly," Tarkovsky
claims the natural world as his ken, and chooses the earth over
the notions of immortality:

If it had been written in the stars
    that I would lie in the cradle of gods
and be raised by a heavenly wet-nurse
    on the holy milk of clouds,

> I'd be the god of a stream or a garden,
> > guard some grain or grave.
> But I don't want to be immortal. I'm human,
> > and scared of an unearthly fate.

Tarkovsky, suffering so much loss, struggles against loss of faith in language—seen vividly in a poem like "I've come to hate them, these words, words, words":

> I've come to hate them, these words, words, words.
> Why should I extol the right
> to rational speech, when branches beat all night
> against the roof, like widows in ragged clothes?

In an interview about this period, Tarkovsky noted:

> Suffering is a constant companion of life. I was only complete-
> ly happy in childhood. But there is a strange way that one
> can accumulate one's strength before reaching great heights.
> I can't tell you how it happens—whether it's necessary to in-
> spire yourself, to learn to see yourself, but a completely hap-
> py man probably cannot write poetry. I wrote the most poems
> in 1952, a very tough year. My wife was sick, and I was very
> afraid for her, wouldn't let anyone come near her, looked
> after her myself. And that very year I wrote a lot. Whatever
> spiritual power I had, it was all put to use.

In a poem as light as "Things"—in which the poet creates an *ubi sunt* of his childhood before the Soviet era—Tarkovsky builds a pathway to a disappeared past, as well as into the future:

> Where is the curly hair of semi-drunk symbolists?
> The scandalous yellow jackets of tall futurists?
> The slogans on lindens and chestnut trees?
> The sawed-off shotguns of crazy thieves?
>
> Those pre-Revolutionary alphabet letters?
> One disappeared, another got altered,
> and what wasn't separated by a comma
> finally found its comma, and died.

I've done so little for the future,
but it's only the future I crave,
and I wouldn't want to start from scratch.
May it turn out I didn't work in vain.

If how we remember the past creates the horizon of the future, then Tarkovsky's memory poems are not exercises in nostalgia—like those lost Cyrillic letters to which he refers in his poem—but a resource of an alternate history.

When Arseny's son Andrei Tarkovsky, the critically-acclaimed international filmmaker, featured his father's voice reading his own poems in films, including *Mirror* (1974) and *Stalker (1979)*, Tarkovsky's poems reached wider audiences. *Mirror* begins with Arseny's "First Times Together," an erotic and spiritual love poem marked by inevitable loss. Its ending contains one of the great voltas in poetry:

Something was leading us.
Built by miracle, whole cities split—
like mirages before our eyes.
And mint bowed beneath our feet,
and birds hovered above our heads,
and fish nosed against the river's flow,
and the sky unscrolled above the land,

while behind us, fate followed
like a madman with a razor in his hand.

Andrei Tarkovsky's vision of filmmaking as "sculpting time" embraced all the arts—poetry, music, painting—in order to merge dream and reality, art and nature. Ingmar Bergman, "[Andrei] Tarkovsky for me is the greatest [director], the one who invented *a new language,* true to the nature of film, as it captures life as a reflection, life as a dream." As Arseny Tarkovsky wrote in a poem from 1977:

I dreamed all this, and this I'm dreaming
and I'll dream this again. Everything

will repeat, and realize its final form
and you will dream whatever I dream.

Beyond us, beyond the world, a wave
beats against the distant shore.
In that wave man rides, and bird, and star,
reality and dreams, and death, wave after wave.

In his final poems, "Gather My Wax When Morning Arrives," Tarkovsky writes some of his most-lasting work, fully realizing his mystical vision. Tarkovsky eulogizes the great poets he knew ("To the Memory of A. A. Akhmatova" and "The Poet"); confronts his war trauma as a way to create a new reason for being ("After the War"); recalls his childhood ("The Suglakleya disappears into the reeds" and "Once Upon A Time"); and begins to bid farewell to his own life ("O, if only I could rise, regain memory and consciousness," "From nowhere at all," and "My sight, which was my power, now blurs"). Even if the old obsessions remain—he continues to swing between insatiable desire and biting remorse, bitter rue and gratitude—the poems are now suffused with prophetic resonance. As early as 1945, Tarkovsky had written about the divine calling of the poet. His poem "The Word" figures words themselves as wombs, and as living beings bearing their own "strange light." That poem ends:

Don't describe too early
Battles or the trials of love.
Refrain from prophecy,
And don't ask for the grave.

A word is only a skin,
A thin film of human lots,
And any line in your poem
Can sharpen the knife of your fate.

Tarkovsky's use of "word" as something more than material language echoes the Gospel of John's "In the beginning was the

Word." Like Anna Akhmatova, Nikolay Gumilev, and Osip Mandelstam before him, Tarkovsky celebrates language as a carrier of national spiritual culture in the face of state propaganda. In a society, as the joke punning on the names of two Soviet newspapers would have it, where "In *Truth* there is no news, and in *News* there is no truth," Tarkovsky's quiet poems ushered forth a way of saying that gained him a wide and devoted readership in Russia.

In contrast to the flashy declamatory political poets that emerged in the post-Stalin Thaw of the 1960s and who have long since lost their relevance, Tarkovsky remains a beloved poet in Russia. His enduring reputation speaks to his poetic labor as the curator and cultivator of words, that ancestral inheritance. As he writes in the poem that concludes this volume:

> I am a candle. I burned at the feast.
> Gather my wax when morning arrives
> so that this page will remind you
> how to be proud, and how to weep,
> how to give away the last third
> of happiness, and to die with ease—
> and beneath a temporary roof
> to burn posthumously, like a word.

Returning to the image from his early poem "Candle"—and in utter tonal contrast to his early existential crisis poem "June 25, 1939"—Tarkovsky offers a vision of a posthumous persistence, a literary flicker of afterlife. Despite bearing so much tragedy, Tarkovsky saw through poetry something that could outlast such unhealable griefs, in the words and the sounds of words—those temporary roofs.

I.

Butterfly in the Hospital Orchard

1926–1945

Свеча

Мерцая жёлтым язычком,
Свеча всё больше оплывает.
Вот так и мы с тобой живём –
Душа горит и тело тает.

1926 г.

Candle

A small yellow tongue flickers.
The candle drips and drips.
This is how you and I live—
our souls flare, flesh disappears.

1926

***

Если б, как прежде, я был горделив,
Я бы оставил тебя навсегда;
Всё, с чем расстаться нельзя ни за что,
Всё, с чем возиться не стоит труда, –
Надвое царство моё разделив.

Я бы сказал:
                              – Ты уносишь с собой
Сто обещаний, сто праздников, сто
Слов. Это можешь с собой унести.

Мне остаётся холодный рассвет,
Сто запоздалых трамваев и сто
Капель дождя на трамвайном пути,
Сто переулков, сто улиц и сто
Капель дождя, побежавших вослед.

25 июня 1934 г.

[If I were the arrogant man I once was]

If I were the arrogant man I once was
I'd leave you forever, leave
what I should never let go,
and everything not worth the grief—
my kingdom divided in two.

I'd say,
                go ahead and seize
one hundred promises, one hundred
holidays, one hundred words. Go ahead.

And I'd be left with a cold dawn, one
hundred late-running trolleys, one hundred
drops of rain on the trolley route,
one hundred lanes, one hundred streets, one
hundred drops of rain running after you.

June 25, 1934

Игнатьевский лес

Последних листьев жар сплошным самосожженьем
Восходит на небо, и на пути твоём
Весь этот лес живёт таким же раздраженьем,
Каким последний год и мы с тобой живём.

В заплаканных глазах отражена дорога,
Как в пойме сумрачной кусты отражены.
Не привередничай, не угрожай, не трогай,
Не задевай лесной наволгшей тишины.

Ты можешь услыхать дыханье старой жизни:
Осклизлые грибы в сырой траве растут,
До самых сердцевин их проточили слизни,
А кожу всё-таки щекочет влажный зуд.

Ты знаешь, как любовь похожа на угрозу, –
Смотри, сейчас вернусь, гляди, убью сейчас!
А небо ёжится и держит клён, как розу, –
Пусть жжёт ещё сильней! – почти у самых глаз.

1935 г.

Ignatievo Forest

The last leaves in self-immolation
burn and rise to sky. The whole forest here
lives and breathes the same irritation
we lived and breathed in our last year.

In your tear-blurred eyes the path's a mirror
as the gloomy flood-plain mirrors the shrubs.
Don't fuss, do not disturb, don't touch
or threaten the wood's wet quiet. Here,

the old life breathes. Just listen:
in damp grass, slimy mushrooms appear.
Slugs gnaw their way to the core,
though a damp itch still tingles the skin.

You've known how love is like a threat:
when I come back, you'll wish you were dead.
The sky shivers in reply, holds a maple like a rose.
Let it burn hotter—till it almost reaches our eyes.

1935

Град на Первой Мещанской

Бьют часы на башне,
Подымается ветер,
Прохожие – в парадные,
Хлопают двери,
По тротуару бегут босоножки,
Дождь за ними гонится,
Бьётся сердце,
Мешает платье,
И розы намокли.

Град
   расшибается вдребезги
     под самой липой...
Всё же
Понемногу отворяются окна,
В серебряной чешуе мостовые,
Дети грызут ледяные орехи.

1935 г.

Hail on First Petit-Bourgeois Street

tongues in the tower
pound the bells to sound
wind lifts   everyone
rushes into entrances   doors
slam   along the sidewalk
bare feet patter   rain chasing
her heart   pounds
her wet dress itches
& the roses are soaked

shatter
          of hail
                    beneath our linden

still
little by little   windows open—
cobblestones slick in silver scales
& children gobble up the nuts of ice

1935

Портрет

Никого со мною нет.
На стене висит портрет.

По слепым глазам старухи
Ходят мухи,
       мухи,
          мухи.

– Хорошо ли, – говорю, –
Под стеклом в твоём раю?

По щеке сползает муха,
Отвечает мне старуха:

– А тебе в твоём дому
Хорошо ли одному?

1937 г.

Portrait

There's no one here
but me. A portrait on the wall—

flies,
      flies,
            flies   crawl
over the old woman's blind eyes.

I ask: Is it nice
under the glass, in your paradise?

Down her cheek, a fly climbs.
The old woman replies:

And you there, in your home—
do you like being alone?

1937

25 июня 1939 года

И страшно умереть, и жаль оставить
Всю шушеру пленительную эту,
Всю чепуху, столь милую поэту,
Которую не удалось прославить.
Я так любил домой прийти к рассвету,
И в полчаса все вещи переставить,
Ещё любил я белый подоконник,
Цветок и воду, и стакан гранёный,
И небосвод голубизны зелёной,
И то, что я – поэт и беззаконник.
А если был июнь и день рожденья,
Боготворил я праздник суетливый,
Стихи друзей и женщин поздравленья,
Хрустальный смех и звон стекла счастливый,
И завиток волос неповторимый,
И этот поцелуй неотвратимый.

Расставлено всё в доме по-другому,
Июнь пришёл, я не томлюсь по дому,
В котором жизнь меня терпенью учит,
И кровь моя мутится в день рожденья,
И тайная меня тревога мучит, –
Что сделал я с высокою судьбою,
О Боже мой, что сделал я с собою!

1939 г.

June 25, 1939

I don't want to die. How could I
leave the magic trifles of life,
all the dear nonsense this poet
never found time to glorify?
How I loved to return at first light,
rearrange the home in dawn's half hour.
I loved the windowsill in white,
the cut glass, the flower in water,
the blue dome of sky gone green,
and, subject to its own law, my poetry.
If it were June and my birthday
I'd worship the bustle of a party—
hugs from women, poems of friends,
crystal laughter, happy clinks of glass,
a curl of hair perfectly out of place,
an inevitable kiss.

It's June, but I don't long for this house
where I'd learned to be patient, to endure.
Everything looks different, out of place.
My birthday's come, and I'm drained of delight,
gnawed by a secret, growing fear—
what have I done with these years?
My God, why have I squandered my life?

1939

***

Стол накрыт на шестерых –
Розы да хрусталь...
А среди гостей моих –
Горе да печаль.

И со мною мой отец,
И со мною брат.
Час проходит. Наконец
У дверей стучат.

Как двенадцать лет назад,
Холодна рука,
И немодные шумят
Синие шелка.

И вино поёт из тьмы,
И звенит стекло:
«Как тебя любили мы,
Сколько лет прошло».

Улыбнётся мне отец,
Брат нальёт вина,
Даст мне руку без колец,
Скажет мне она:

«Каблучки мои в пыли,
Выцвела коса,
И звучат из-под земли
Наши голоса».

1940 г.

[The table is set for six]

The table is set for six,
all roses and crystal.
Among my guests,
Grief and Loss mingle.

First my father,
and now my brother,
come to pass the hour.
A knock at the door:

Like twelve years ago, her hand,
still cold to the touch.
Her silks, blue and old-fashioned,
still rustle and swish.

From the dark, the wine sings
and the crystal rings:
How much we loved you,
how many winters ago.

My father would smile at me,
my brother, pour some wine.
Her ringless hand in mine,
the woman would say:

My heels are caked with dirt,
my plaited hair's gone clear,
and our voices now call out
from under the earth.

1940

Сверчок

Если правду сказать,
      я по крови – домашний сверчок,
Заповедную песню
      пою над печною золой,
И один для меня
      приготовит крутой кипяток,
А другой для меня
      приготовит шесток золотой.

Путешественник вспомнит
      мой голос в далёком краю,
Даже если меня
      променяет на знойных цикад.
Сам не знаю, кто выстругал
      бедную скрипку мою,
Знаю только, что песнями
      я, как цикада, богат.

Сколько русских согласных
      в полночном моём языке,
Сколько я поговорок
      сложил в коробок лубяной,
Чтобы шарили дети
      в моём лубяном коробке,
В старой скрипке запечной
      с единственной медной струной.

Ты не слышишь меня,
      голос мой – как часы за стеной,
А прислушайся только –
      и я поведу за собой,

The Cricket

To tell the truth, I'm kin
          to the house cricket.
I sing a secret song
          upon the oven's ash.
For me, one brings
          the water to a fierce boil,
for me, another
          prepares a hearth of gold.

A traveler will recall
          my voice in a distant land,
even if he's traded
          me for the heat cicada.
I don't know who planed
          my creaky violin,
but I know that I'm rich
          in songs as a cicada.

How many Russian consonants
          in my midnight language,
how many sayings
          I place in the bast box
so a child can rummage
          in my living violin,
with my one brass string,
          hidden behind the oven.

You can't really hear me,
          my voice like a clock
behind a wall, but take heed
          and I'll lead you.

Я весь дом подыму:
       просыпайтесь, я сторож ночной!
И заречье твоё
       отзовётся сигнальной трубой.

1940 г.

I'll rouse the whole house:
        I'm the night watchman. Arise!
Your people across the river
        will trumpet their reply.

1940

***

С утра я тебя дожидался вчера,
Они догадались, что ты не придёшь,
Ты помнишь, какая погода была?
Как в праздник! И я выходил без пальто.

Сегодня пришла, и устроили нам
Какой-то особенно пасмурный день,
И дождь, и особенно поздний час,
И капли бегут по холодным ветвям.

Ни словом унять, ни платком утереть...

1941 г.

[Yesterday morning I began waiting for you]

Yesterday morning I began waiting for you
and would, until dark. They somehow knew
you would not come. Remember the festive weather?
I kept heading outside, without a coat, to wait.

Today you've finally arrived, and they've made us
an especially gloomy day. It's raining
and gray, and now too late.
Drop after drop glides down cold branches.

A word will not stop them. No hand will wipe them away.

1941

Из «Чистопольской тетради»

II.

Беспомощней, суровее и суше
Я духом стал под бременем несчастий.
В последний раз ты говоришь о страсти,
Не страсть, а скорбь терзает наши души.

Пред дикими заклятьями кликуши
Не вздрогнет мир, разорванный на части.
Что стоит плач, что может звон запястий,
Когда свистит загробный ветер в уши?

В кромешном шуме рокового боя
Не слышно клятв, а слово бесполезно.
Я не бессмертен, ты, как тень, мгновенна.

Нет больше ни приюта, ни покоя,
Ни ангела над пропастью беззвездной.
А ты одна, одна во всей Вселенной.

7 ноября 1941 г.

From "Chistopol Notebook"

II.

Under the yoke of bad luck
I've become helpless, brittle, and hard.
For the last time you speak of lust.
Not lust. It's grief that torments us.

The shrieking pledges of a prophet
won't remake a world torn apart.
What's the point of ringing bracelets, or tears,
with the wind of graves in our ears?

The tornado of fated battle
drowns out all promises. Words fail.
You're a momentary ghost, I'm not immortal.

There's nothing left: neither shelter nor peace,
nor an angel over the starless abyss,
and you're alone, alone in the universe.

November 7, 1941

IV. Беженец

Не пожалела на дорогу соли,
Так насолила, что свела с ума.
Горишь, святая камская зима,
А я живу один, как ветер в поле.

Скупишься, мать, дала бы хлеба, что ли,
Полны ядрёным снегом закрома,
Бери да ешь. Тяжка моя сума:
Полпуда горя и ломоть недоли.

Я ноги отморожу на ветру,
Я беженец, я никому не нужен,
Тебе-то всё равно, а я умру.

Что делать мне среди твоих жемчужин
И кованного стужей серебра
На чёрной Каме, ночью, без костра?

13 ноября 1941 г.

IV. Refugee

You granted me some salt for the journey,
sprinkled so much white I lost my mind.
Holy Kama winter, you burn like light.
I live alone as wind in a winter field.

You're stingy, Mother. Just give me
a little bread. The silos are filled
with snow. I'm hungry. My bag is heavy:
A loaf of sorrow for a bite of catastrophe.

The frost is gnawing my feet.
Who needs me? I'm a refugee.
You don't care whether or not I breathe.

What should I do among your pearls
and the chill wrought silver
on the black Kama, at night, without a fire?

November 13, 1941

V.

Дровяные, погонные возвожу алтари.
Кама, Кама, река моя, полыньи свои отвори.

Всё, чем татары хвастали, красавица, покажи,
Наточенные ножи да затопленные баржи.

Окаю, гибель кличу, баланду кипячу,
Каторжную тачку, матерясь, качу,

С возчиками, грузчиками пью твоё вино,
По доске скрипучей сойду на чёрное дно.

Кама, Кама, чем я плачу за твою ледяную парчу?
Я за твою парчу верной смертью плачу.

15 ноября 1941 г.

V.

I'm piling up lines of firewood altars
to thaw your icy glare, Kama, my river.

My beauty, show us what makes the Tartars brag,
from sharpened knives to sunken barges.

I drawl like a local, I wail for death, boil some swill,
and haul around my prison barrow, cursing at will.

With the loaders and drivers, I'll drink your draughts.
I'll fall from a creaky board to your black depths.

Kama, Kama, how can I pay for your frozen brocade?
I'd pay with my death.

November 15, 1941

VII.

Нестерпимо во гневе караешь, Господь,
Стыну я под дыханьем твоим,
Ты людскую мою беззащитную плоть
Рассекаешь мечом ледяным.

Вьюжный ангел мне молотом пальцы дробит
На закате Судного дня,
И целует в глаза, и в уши трубит,
И снегами заносит меня.

Я дышать не могу под твоей стопой,
Я вином твоим пыточным пьян.
Кто я, Господи Боже мой, перед тобой?
Себастьян, твой слуга Себастьян.

18 ноября 1941 г.

VII.

In anger you punish unbearably, Lord,
and I freeze beneath your breath,
you dissect with an icy sword
my defenseless human flesh.

On Judgment Day, as night falls,
the blizzard-angel hammers apart
my fingers, kisses my eyes, blows
a trumpet in my ears, palls me in snow.

I cannot breathe beneath your foot.
I'm drunk on your torture—your wine.
Who am I, before you, O Lord?
Sebastian, thy servant, Sebastian.

November 18, 1941

VIII.

Упала, задохнулась на бегу,
Огнём горит твой город златоглавый,
А всё платочек комкаешь кровавый,
Всё маешься, недужная, в снегу.

Я не ревную к моему врагу,
Я не страшусь твоей недоброй славы,
Кляни меня, замучь, но – Боже правый! –
Любить тебя в обиде не могу.

Не птицелов раскидывает сети,
Сетями воздух стал в твой смертный час,
Нет для тебя живой воды на свете.

Когда Господь от гибели не спас,
Как я спасу, как полюблю – такую?
О нет, очнись, я гибну и тоскую...

28 ноября 1941 г.

VIII.

You ran, choking, until you fell.
Your gold-domed city burning down,
your bloody handkerchief crumpled,
you waste away, sick, in the snow.

I'm not jealous of my enemy,
not afraid of your notoriety.
Curse me, torture me, but my God,
I can't love you just because you hurt.

No fowlers spread out their nets; the very air
was like a net at the hour of your death.
The water of life had fled the earth.

If God could not save you from the grave,
how could I? How could I fall in love?
Wake up. Come back. I'm dying of grief.

November 28, 1941

X.

Зову – не отзывается, крепко спит Марина.
Елабуга, Елабуга, кладбищенская глина,

Твоим бы именем назвать гиблое болото,
Таким бы словом, как засовом, запирать ворота,

Тобою бы, Елабуга, детей стращать немилых,
Купцам бы да разбойникам лежать в твоих могилах.

А на кого дохнула ты холодом лютым?
Кому была последним земным приютом?

Чей слышала перед зарей возглас лебединый?
Ты слышала последнее слово Марины.

На гибельном ветру твоём я тоже стыну.
Еловая, проклятая, отдай Марину!

28 ноября 1941 г.

X.

I call, but Marina does not reply. She sleeps today
so soundly in Yelabuga. Yelabuga, cemetery clay,

You should be called a god-forgotten bog.
At your name, like a bolt, the gates should be locked.

Yelabuga, you'd have no trouble scaring orphans.
Swindlers and robbers should lie in your coffins.

On whom did you breathe your fierce frost,
becoming her final earthly rest?

Whose swan's cry did you hear before dawn?
Tsvetaeva's. You heard Marina's last word.

I'm freezing in your cemetery wind.
Cursed, spruce-stabbed Yelabuga, give back Marina.

November 28, 1941

Белый день

Камень лежит у жасмина.
Под этим камнем клад.
Отец стоит на дорожке.
Белый-белый день.

В цвету серебристый тополь,
Центифолия, а за ней –
Вьющиеся розы,
Молочная трава.

Никогда я не был
Счастливей, чем тогда.
Никогда я не был
Счастливей, чем тогда.

Вернуться туда невозможно
И рассказать нельзя,
Как был переполнен блаженством
Этот райский сад.

1942 г.

Beautiful Day

Beneath the jasmine a stone
marks a buried treasure.
On the path, my father stands.
A beautiful, beautiful day.

The gray poplar blooms,
centifolia blooms,
and milky grass,
and behind it, roses climb.

I have never been
more happy than then.
I have never been more
happy than then.

To return is impossible
and to talk about it, forbidden—
how it was filled with bliss,
that heavenly garden.

1942

***

Здесь дом стоял. Жил в нём какой-то дед.
Жил какой-то мальчик. Больше дома нет.

Бомба в сто кило, земля черным-черна,
Был дом, нет дома. Что делать, война!

Куча серых тряпок, на ней самовар,
Шкафчик, рядом лошадь, над лошадью пар.

Вырастет на пустыре лебеда у стены.
Здесь навсегда поселятся бедные духи войны.

А то без них некому будет скулить по ночам,
Свистеть да гулять по нетопленым печам.

1942 г.

[Here, a house once stood. Inside, some old man]

Here, a house once stood. Inside, some old man
lived with a child. And now the house is gone.

A hundred kilo bomb—the earth, blacker than black.
A home, now none. That's war; what can be done?

On a heap of gray rags, a samovar gleams.
A dresser, nearby a horse. Above the horse, steam.

Along the ruined wall, some goosefoot weeds will grow.
The wretched ghosts of war will make a home

right here, forever. Without them, who would moan
at night, whistle and writhe in unheated stoves?

1942

***

Немецкий автоматчик подстрелит на дороге,
Осколком ли фугаски перешибут мне ноги,

В живот ли пулю влепит эсэсовец-мальчишка,
Но всё равно мне будет на этом фронте крышка.

И буду я разутый, без имени и славы
Замёрзшими глазами смотреть на снег кровавый.

1942 г.

[A German machinegunner will shoot me in the road, or]

A German machinegunner will shoot me in the road, or
a detonation bomb will break my legs, or

an SS-boy will slam a bullet in my gut—
in any case, on this front, they've got me covered.

Without my name, or glory, or even boots—
with frozen eyes, I'll gaze at the snow, blood-colored.

1942

***

Стояла батарея за этим вот холмом,
Нам ничего не слышно, а здесь остался гром,
Под этим снегом трупы ещё лежат вокруг,
И в воздухе морозном остались взмахи рук.
Ни шагу знаки смерти ступить нам не дают.
Сегодня снова, снова убитые встают.
Сейчас они услышат, как снегири поют.

1942 г.

[The gun battery was over there, behind that hill]

The gun battery was over there, behind that hill.
We cannot hear it, but its thunder remains still,
around us, the corpses lie beneath the snow,
and in the icy air, their arms are still flailing.
Who would dare to trample this field now?
Today, the dead ones rise again. Now they will
hear the red-breasted snowbird sing.

1942

***

Ехал из Брянска в теплушке слепой,
Ехал домой со своею судьбой.

Что-то ему говорила она,
Только и слов – слепота и война.

Мол, хорошо, что незряч да убог,
Был бы ты зряч, уцелеть бы не мог.

Немец не тронул, на что ты ему?
Дай-ка на плечи надену суму,

Ту ли худую, пустую суму,
Дай-ка я веки тебе подыму.

Ехал слепой со своею судьбой,
Даром что слеп, а доволен собой.

1943 г.

[A blind man was riding an unheated train]

A blind man was riding an unheated train,
from Bryansk he was traveling home with his fate.

Fate whispered to him so the whole car could hear:
and why should you worry over blindness and war?

It's good, she was saying, you're sightless and poor.
If you were not blind, you'd never survive.

The Germans won't kill you; you're nothing to them.
Let me lift the bag to your shoulder—

the one over there, empty and ripped.
Allow me to lift up your eyelids.

The blind man was traveling home with his fate,
now thankful for blindness. Happy with it.

1943

***

Не стой тут,
Убьют.
Воздух! Ложись!
Проклятая жизнь!
Милая жизнь!
Странная смутная жизнь!
Дикая жизнь!
Травы мои коленчатые,
Мои луговые бабочки,
Небо – всё в облаках, городах, лагунах
и парусных лодках!
Дай мне ещё подышать,
Дай мне побыть в этой жизни безумной
и жадной,
Хмельному от водки,
С пистолетом в руках
Ждать танков немецких,
Дай мне побыть хоть в этом окопе…

1943 г.

[Don't stand here]

Don't stand here
or you'll get smeared.
Incoming! Get down!
This damned,
this darling,
indiscernable
untameable life.
O, knobby-kneed grasses,
my meadow butterflies,
sky all cloudbanks, towns, lagoons,
                    and sailboats!
Let me breathe a little longer.
Greedy life, let me stay
                    just a little longer,
hungover from vodka,
pistol in my hand,
waiting for German tanks—
even in this trench, just let me exist.

1943

Западное небо

На полоски несжатого хлеба
Золотые ладьи низошли.
Как ты близко, закатное небо,
От моей опалённой земли.

Каждый парус твой розов и тонок, –
Отвори нам степные пути,
Помоги от траншей и воронок
До прохлады твоей добрести.

10 августа 1943 г.

Western Sky

On patches of unreaped rye
boats of gold descend.
How close you come, evening sky,
to my scorched steppe.

Your sails so pink and delicate.
Chart a new course
from trenches and bomb craters,
draw us to your gentle waters.

August 10, 1943

Охота

Охота кончается.
Меня затравили.
Борзая висит у меня на бедре.
Закинул я голову так, что рога упёрлись
в лопатки.
Трублю.
Подрезают мне сухожилья.
В ухо тычут ружейным стволом.

Падает на бок, цепляясь рогами за мокрые прутья.
Вижу я тусклое око с какой-то налипшей травинкой.
Чёрное, окостеневшее яблоко без отражений.
Ноги свяжут и шест проденут, вскинут на плечи...

1944 г.

The Hunt

　　is done
　　I'm trapped
　　a hound hanging on my thigh
　　I throw my head back until my horns rest on
　　　　my shoulders
　　I trumpet
　　as they slash my tendons
　　and jab a rifle in my ear

He falls on his side, his antlers clinging to wet twigs.
I can see his dim eye, a blade of grass stuck to it.
A stiffened black apple, reflecting nothing.

They'll bind the legs together, pass a pole through, and toss it
　　over their shoulders.

1944

Бабочка в госпитальном саду

Из тени в свет перелетая,
Она сама и тень и свет,
Где родилась она такая,
Почти лишённая примет?
Она летает, приседая,
Она, должно быть, из Китая,
Здесь на неё похожих нет,
Она из тех забытых лет,
Где капля малая лазори
Как море синее во взоре.

Она клянется: навсегда! –
Не держит слова никогда,
Она едва до двух считает,
Не понимает ничего,
Из целой азбуки читает
Две гласных буквы –

                    А
                    и
                    О.
А имя бабочки – рисунок,
Нельзя произнести его,
И для чего ей быть в покое?
Она как зеркальце простое.

Пожалуйста, не улетай,
О госпожа моя, в Китай!
Не надо, не ищи Китая,
Из тени в свет перелетая.
Душа, зачем тебе Китай?
О госпожа моя цветная,
Пожалуйста, не улетай!

1945 г.

Butterfly in the Hospital Orchard

Flying from shadow into the light,
she is herself both shadow and light.
Where did she come from, this being
nearly naked of markings?
She looks like she's hopping.
She must be from Asia—
there's no one quite like her here.
She must be from forgotten years,
where a tincture of azure
is a blue sea in our eyes.

She swears it will be forever
but keeps the word *never.*
She can hardly count to two,
understands little,
and from the whole alphabet knows
only two vowels—

A

&

O.

The butterfly's name is a picture
impossible to pronounce. And why
does she have to be so quiet?
She's too much a mirror.

Don't fly off to the East, O,
my lady! Don't chase the East,
flying from shadows
into the light. My soul, why
do you long for a far-off place?
O my colorful beloved, my
darling, don't fly away.

1945

Иванова ива

Иван до войны проходил у ручья,
Где выросла ива неведомо чья.

Не знали, зачем на ручей налегла,
А это Иванова ива была.

В своей плащ-палатке, убитый в бою,
Иван возвратился под иву свою.

Иванова ива,
Иванова ива,
Как белая лодка, плывёт по ручью.

1958 г.

Valya's Willow

Before the war Valya walked along the creek,
where a willow grew for who knows who.

Though why it stood on the creek, no one knew.
Valya owned that willow.

Killed in action, Valya came back
under his willow in his military cloak.

Valya's willow,
Valya's willow,
like a white boat floating on the creek.

1958

Суббота, 21 июня

Пусть роют щели хоть под воскресенье.
В моих руках надежда на спасенье.

Как я хотел вернуться в до-войны,
Предупредить, кого убить должны.

Мне вон тому сказать необходимо:
«Иди сюда, и смерть промчится мимо».

Я знаю час, когда начнут войну,
Кто выживет, и кто умрёт в плену,

И кто из нас окажется героем,
И кто расстрелян будет перед строем,

И сам я видел вражеских солдат,
Уже заполонивших Сталинград,

И видел я, как русская пехота
Штурмует Бранденбургские ворота.

Что до врага, то всё известно мне,
Как ни одной разведке на войне.

Я говорю – не слушают, не слышат,
Несут цветы, субботним ветром дышат,

Уходят, пропусков не выдают,
В домашний возвращаются уют.

Saturday, June 21st, 1941

Let them dig trenches, though it's nearly the end
of spring. The hope for salvation's in my hands.

How I want to return to the days before battle,
to warn the ones who will be killed.

I feel the urge to say to that person over there:
"Your death will whistle past if you stand here."

I know the hour when they'll begin the war,
who'll survive and who'll die a prisoner,

and who of us will turn into a hero,
and who will be shot in front of his formation,

and now I see the enemy troops, a horde,
I see them swarming toward Stalingrad.

And now I see the Russian infantry gather, wait
like clouds, then storm the Brandenburg Gates.

About the enemy, I have complete information
better than any reconnaissance from the front.

I'm speaking, but no one hears, or listens—
they carry flowers, inhale the Saturday wind,

they take leave, and need no special permit,
returning to their homes and their comfort.

И я уже не помню сам, откуда
Пришёл сюда и что случилось чудо.

Я всё забыл. В окне ещё светло,
И накрест не заклеено стекло.

1945 г.

And I've forgotten how I came here,
that a miracle has occurred. I remember

nothing. Light still shines through unbroken glass—
the windows not yet covered by paper crosses.

1945

Полевой госпиталь

Стол повернули к свету. Я лежал
Вниз головой, как мясо на весах,
Душа моя на нитке колотилась,
И видел я себя со стороны:
Я без довесков был уравновешен
Базарной жирной гирей.
        Это было
Посередине снежного щита,
Щербатого по западному краю,
В кругу незамерзающих болот,
Деревьев с перебитыми ногами
И железнодорожных полустанков
С расколотыми черепами, чёрных
От снежных шапок, то двойных, а то
Тройных.
        В тот день остановилось время,
Не шли часы, и души поездов
По насыпям не пролетали больше
Без фонарей, на серых ластах пара,
И ни вороньих свадеб, ни метелей,
Ни оттепелей не было в том лимбе,
Где я лежал в позоре, в наготе,
В крови своей, вне поля тяготенья
Грядущего.
Но сдвинулся и на оси пошёл
По кругу щит слепительного снега,
И низко у меня над головой
Семёрка самолетов развернулась,
И марля, как древесная кора,
На теле затвердела, и бежала
Чужая кровь из колбы в жилы мне,
И я дышал, как рыба на песке,

Field Hospital

The table was turned to light. I lay
my head down like meat on a scale,
my soul throbbing on a thread.
I could see myself from above:
I would have been balanced
by a stout market weight.
                        I lay
in the middle of the snowy shield
pocked along its western side,
in a circle of never-freezing swamps,
forests with fractured legs
and the split skulls
of railway stations,
their snowy pates blackened
over and again.
                        On that day,
the clocks stopped, souls of trains
no longer flew along lampless levies,
upon the gray fins of steam;
neither crow weddings nor snowstorms
nor thaws penetrated this limbo
where I lay in disgrace, naked,
in my own blood, outside the future's
magnetic pull.
But then the wheel of blinding snow
shifted and began to turn on its axle,
and a wedge of seven planes flew low
over my head, turning back,
and gauze grew hard as tree bark
all over my body, and another's
blood flowed into my veins, and
I breathed like a fish on sand,

Глотая твёрдый, слюдяной, земной,
Холодный и благословенный воздух.

Мне губы обметало, и ещё
Меня поили с ложки, и ещё
Не мог я вспомнить, как меня зовут,
Но ожил у меня на языке
Словарь царя Давида. А потом
И снег сошёл, и ранняя весна
На цыпочки привстала и деревья
Окутала своим платком зелёным.

1964 г.

swallowing the hard, mica-flecked,
cold and blessed air.

My lips were covered with sores, and also
I was fed by a spoon, and also
I could not remember my name,
but the language of King David came
alive on my tongue.
                    And then
even the snow disappeared,
and early spring, rising on tiptoes,
draped her green scarf over the trees.

1964

II.

The Earthly Feast

1945–1965

Книга травы

О нет, я не город с кремлём над рекой,
Я разве что герб городской.

Не герб городской, а звезда над щитком
На этом гербе городском.

Не гостья небесная в черни воды,
Я разве что имя звезды.

Не голос, не платье на том берегу,
Я только светиться могу.

Не луч световой у тебя за спиной,
Я – дом, разорённый войной.

Не дом на высоком валу крепостном,
Я – память о доме твоём.

Не друг твой, судьбою ниспосланный друг,
Я – выстрела дальнего звук.

В приморскую степь я тебя уведу,
На влажную землю паду,

И стану я книгой младенческих трав,
К родимому лону припав.

1945 г.

The Book of Grass

I'm not a walled city above a river,
I'm the city's coat of arms.

Not the city's coat of arms, I'm a star above the shield
on the city's coat of arms.

Not that heavenly visitor in a blackness of water,
I'm the name of the star.

Not a voice, not a dress on that far shore—
I can only shine.

Not a ray of light beyond your vision,
I'm a house in ruins from the war.

Not a house on the high rampart,
I'm the memory of your home.

O, not your friend, the one who's sent by fate;
I'm the sound of a distant shot.

I lead you to the steppe along the coast
and lie down on the humid earth.

I become the book of newborn grass
as I nuzzle into the native womb.

1945

Слово

Слово только оболочка,
Плёнка, звук пустой, но в нём
Бьётся розовая точка,
Странным светится огнём,

Бьётся жилка, вьётся живчик,
А тебе и дела нет,
Что в сорочке твой счастливчик
Появляется на свет.

Власть от века есть у слова,
И уж если ты поэт,
И когда пути другого
У тебя на свете нет,

Не описывай заране
Ни сражений, ни любви,
Опасайся предсказаний,
Смерти лучше не зови!

Слово только оболочка,
Плёнка жребиев людских,
На тебя любая строчка
Точит нож в стихах твоих.

1945 г.

The Word

A word is only a skin, thin
film, an empty sound, but inside
a pink point is beating,
shining like a strange light.

A vein pulses, an artery swirls.
And you don't care at all,
the lucky one you've found
has been born with a caul.

From the beginning, the word
was power. If you're a poet
and have no better path
in this tangled world,

don't describe too early
battles or the trials of love.
Refrain from prophecy,
and don't ask for the grave.

A word is only a skin,
a thin film of human lots,
and any line in your poem
can sharpen the knife of your fate.

1945

***

Я учился траве, раскрывая тетрадь,
И трава начинала как флейта звучать.
Я ловил соответствия звука и цвета,
И когда запевала свой гимн стрекоза,
Меж зелёных ладов проходя, как комета,
Я-то знал, что любая росинка – слеза.
Знал, что в каждой фасетке огромного ока,
В каждой радуге яркострекочущих крыл
Обитает горящее слово пророка,
И Адамову тайну я чудом открыл.

Я любил свой мучительный труд, эту кладку
Слов, скреплённых их собственным светом, загадку
Смутных чувств и простую разгадку ума,
В слове *правда* мне виделась правда сама,
Был язык мой правдив, как спектральный анализ,
А слова у меня под ногами валялись.

И ещё я скажу: собеседник мой прав,
В четверть шума я слышал, в полсвета я видел,
Но зато не унизил ни близких, ни трав,
Равнодушием отчей земли не обидел,
И пока на земле я работал, приняв
Дар студёной воды и пахучего хлеба,
Надо мною стояло бездонное небо,
Звёзды падали мне на рукав.

1956 г.

[I learned the grass as I began to write]

I learned the grass as I began to write,
and the grass started whistling like a flute.
I gathered how color and sound could join,
and when the dragonfly whirred up his hymn—
passing through green frets like a comet—
I knew a tear in each drop of dew.
Knew that in each facet of the huge eye,
in each rainbow of brightly churring wings,
dwells the burning word of the prophet—
by some miracle I found Adam's secret.

I loved my tormenting task, this intricate
positioning of words, fastened by their light,
riddle of vague feeling and a sudden clarity
alighting. In *truth* I thought truth appeared.
My tongue was true, like a spectral analysis,
and words gathered around my feet to listen.

What's more, my friend, you're right to say
I heard one-quarter the noise, saw half the light.
But I did not debase the grasses, or my family,
or insult the ancestral earth by being blithe,
and as long as I worked on earth, accepted
a gift of coldest spring water and fragrant bread,
above me, the abyssal sky leaned down
and stars tumbled, hurtling toward this hand.

1956

Вещи

Всё меньше тех вещей, среди которых
Я в детстве жил, на свете остаётся.
Где лампы-«молнии»? Где чёрный порох?
Где чёрная вода со дна колодца?

Где «Остров мёртвых» в декадентской раме?
Где плюшевые красные диваны?
Где фотографии мужчин с усами?
Где тростниковые аэропланы?

Где Надсона чахоточный трехдольник,
Визитки на красавцах-адвокатах,
Пахучие калоши «Треугольник»
И страусова нега плеч покатых?

Где кудри символистов полупьяных?
Где рослых футуристов затрапезы?
Где лозунги на липах и каштанах,
Бандитов сумасшедшие обрезы?

Где твёрдый знак и буква «ять» с «фитою»?
Одно ушло, другое изменилось,
И что не отделялось запятою,
То запятой и смертью отделилось.

Я сделал для грядущего так мало,
Но только по грядущему тоскую
И не желаю начинать сначала:
Быть может, я работал не впустую.

Things

They grow more and more scarce, the things
that haunt this earth since I was young.
Where are the lightning lamps? The black powder?
Where is the well-bottom's sweet black water,

the decadently-framed "Isle of the Dead"?
Where are the plush red settees?
Where are the photos of moustached men?
Where are the airplanes built from reeds?

And Nadson's consumptive measures?
The morning coats on handsome lawyers?
Triangle Company's smelly galoshes?
And the ostrich bliss of bowed shoulders?

Where is the curly hair of semi-drunk symbolists?
The scandalous yellow jackets of tall futurists?
The slogans on linden and chestnut trees?
The sawed-off shotguns of crazy thieves?

Those pre-revolutionary alphabet letters?
One disappeared, another got altered,
and what wasn't separated by a comma
finally found its comma, and died.

I've done so little for the future,
but it's only the future I crave,
and I wouldn't want to start from scratch.
May it turn out I didn't work in vain.

А где у новых спутников порука,
Что мне принадлежат они по праву?
Я посягаю на игрушки внука,
Хлеб правнуков, праправнукову славу.

1957 г.

All these new fellow travelers—
do I have any real claim to them?
I stumble over my grandson's toys, and plunder
great-grandchildren's bread, my great-great-grandson's fame.

1957

***

Я прощаюсь со всем, чем когда-то я был
И что я презирал, ненавидел, любил.

Начинается новая жизнь для меня,
И прощаюсь я с кожей вчерашнего дня.

Больше я от себя не желаю вестей
И прощаюсь с собою до мозга костей,

И уже, наконец, над собою стою,
Отделяю постылую душу мою,

В пустоте оставляю себя самого,
Равнодушно смотрю на себя – на него.

Здравствуй, здравствуй, моя ледяная броня,
Здравствуй, хлеб без меня и вино без меня,

Сновидения ночи и бабочки дня,
Здравствуй, всё без меня и вы все без меня!

Я читаю страницы неписаных книг,
Слышу круглого яблока круглый язык,

Слышу белого облака белую речь,
Но ни слова для вас не умею сберечь,

Потому что сосудом скудельным я был
И не знаю, зачем сам себя я разбил.

[I bid farewell to everything I was]

I bid farewell to everything I was,
everything I despised, disliked, and loved.

And now, a new life begins,
I bid farewell to yesterday's skin.

About me, I no longer need any news.
I bid goodbye—right to the marrow.

At last, I look down on what I was,
see my separate soul, no longer loved,

and gaze with calm at myself, at him,
and leave them alone in the abyss.

Hello, hello, my armor of ice.
Hello, bread and not me. Hello, wine.

Dreams of night and butterflies of day,
hello, everything and everyone without me.

I read the pages of unwritten novels,
I hear the round language of a round apple,

I hear the white speech of a white cloud,
but cannot save for you even a word

because I was the weaker vessel.
I don't know why I broke myself.

Больше сферы подвижной в руке не держу
И ни слова без слова я вам не скажу.

А когда-то во мне находили слова
Люди, рыбы и камни, листва и трава.

1957 г.

I won't hold in my hand the turning sphere,
won't say to you a word without a word.

Yet long ago, the fish and rocks and leaves
and people and grass found their words in me.

1957

***

Вечерний, сизокрылый,
Благословенный свет!
Я словно из могилы
Смотрю тебе вослед.

Благодарю за каждый
Глоток воды живой,
В часы последней жажды
Подаренный тобой.

За каждое движенье
Твоих прохладных рук,
За то, что утешенья
Не нахожу вокруг.

За то, что ты надежды
Уводишь, уходя,
И ткань твоей одежды
Из ветра и дождя.

1958 г.

[You evening light, gray]

You evening light, gray-
winged and blessed light—
as though from the grave
I follow you with my eyes,

grateful for this taste
of fabled elixir
in the hours of final thirst
that you deliver.

For your cool hands,
and the way they flutter,
for how I cannot find
consolation anywhere.

For gathering up all hope
when you leave again,
for the stitch of your clothes
made of wind and rain.

1958

Из окна

Ещё мои руки не связаны,
Глаза не взглянули в последний,
Последние рифмы не сказаны,
Не пахнет венками в передней.

Наверчены звёздные линии
На северном полюсе мира,
И прямоугольная, синяя
В окно моё вдвинута лира.

А ниже – бульвары и здания
В кристальном скрипичном напеве, –
Как будущее, как сказание,
Как Будда у матери в чреве.

1958 г.

From the Window

These hands are not yet bound,
these eyes have yet to cast their last—
my final rhymes have yet to sound
and no burial wreaths perfume the house.

Starry lines wind and spire
around the globe's northern pole,
and a sky-blue rectangular lyre
thrusts through my window.

Below, the boulevards and buildings,
a crystal violin tune—
like the future, like folk songs,
like Buddha in his mother's womb.

1958

* * *

Пускай меня простит Винсент Ван-Гог
За то, что я помочь ему не мог,

За то, что я травы ему под ноги
Не постелил на выжженной дороге,

За то, что я не развязал шнурков
Его крестьянских пыльных башмаков,

За то, что в зной не дал ему напиться,
Не помешал в больнице застрелиться.

Стою себе, а надо мной навис
Закрученный, как пламя, кипарис,

Лимонный крон и тёмно-голубое, –
Без них не стал бы я самим собою;

Унизил бы я собственную речь,
Когда б чужую ношу сбросил с плеч.

А эта грубость ангела, с какою
Он свой мазок роднит с моей строкою,

Ведёт и вас через его зрачок
Туда, где дышит звёздами Ван-Гог.

1958 г.

[May Vincent van Gogh forgive me]

May Vincent van Gogh forgive me
for not helping him—that I did not

spread leaves beneath his feet
on the burning road, that I did not

untie the laces of his dusty boots,
that I did not give him, in the raging heat,

anything to drink and did not stop him,
in the hospital, from ending his life.

I stand here and lift my eyes
to the cypress, twisting like a flame.

That lemon-yellow, that deep blue—I
wouldn't have become myself without them.

I would have debased my own words
if I'd shrugged off his burden.

And the coarse angel that connects
his brushstrokes to my lines, leads

you, too, through the depths of seeing,
where Vincent van Gogh breathes stars.

1958

Поэты

Мы звёзды меняем на птичьи кларнеты
И флейты, пока ещё живы поэты,
И флейты – на синие щётки цветов,
Трещотки стрекоз и кнуты пастухов.

Как странно подумать, что мы променяли
На рифмы, в которых так много печали,
На голос, в котором и присвист и жесть,
Свою корневую, подземную честь.

А вы нас любили, а вы нас хвалили,
Так что ж вы лежите могила к могиле
И молча плывёте, в ладьях накренясь,
Косарь и псалтырщик, и плотничий князь?

1958 г.

Poets

While poets still live we trade the stars
for clarinets and flutes of birds;
and flutes, for blue brushes of flowers,
ratchets of dragonflies, whips of shepherds.

How strange to think that we've exchanged
for rhyme—in which there's so much sorrow—
for voice—its sibilation and terror—
our rooted-underground honor.

And you've loved us, and us you've praised,
so why do you lie there, grave to grave
and float mute in boats, listing—
scyther and psalmist and carpenter prince?

1958

Оливы

Марине Т.

Дорога ведёт под обрыв,
Где стала трава на колени
И призраки диких олив,
На камни рога положив,
Застыли, как стадо оленей.
Мне странно, что я ещё жив
Средь стольких могил и видений.

Я сторож вечерних часов
И серой листвы надо мною.
Осеннее небо мой кров.
Не помню я собственных снов
И слёз твоих поздних не стою.
Давно у меня за спиною
Задвинут железный засов.

А где-то судьба моя прячет
Ключи у степного костра,
И спутник её до утра
В багровой рубахе маячит.
Ключи она прячет и плачет
О том, что ей песня сестра
И в путь собираться пора.

Седые оливы, рога мне
Кладите на плечи теперь,
Кладите рога, как на камни:
Святой колыбелью была мне
Земля похорон и потерь.

1958 г.

The Olive Trees

for Marina Tarkovskaya

The road leads down a cliff
where grass falls to its knees,
and ghosts of wild olive,
their antlers growing on stones,
are frozen like a herd of deer.
I'm surprised I'm still alive
amid so many graves and visions.

I guard the evening hours
and the gray foliage above me.
The autumn sky is my shelter.
I don't remember my own dreams;
I'm unworthy of your late tears.
An epoch has passed since the iron bar
invisibly locked the door.

And somewhere my fate hides
the keys near a steppe fire,
her flickering companion looming
in a red shirt until morning.
She hides them and laments
the song of her sibling
and that the song will end.

Gray olive trees, lift your horns
onto my shoulders
as if I were of stone.
This is my sacred cradle—
this land of loss and funerals.

1958

Малютка-жизнь

Я жизнь люблю и умереть боюсь.
Взглянули бы, как я под током бьюсь
И гнусь, как язь в руках у рыболова,
Когда я перевоплощаюсь в слово.

Но я не рыба и не рыболов.
И я из обитателей углов,
Похожий на Раскольникова с виду.
Как скрипку я держу свою обиду.

Терзай меня – не изменюсь в лице.
Жизнь хороша, особенно в конце,
Хоть под дождём и без гроша в кармане,
Хоть в Судный день – с иголкою в гортани.

А! Этот сон! Малютка-жизнь, дыши,
Возьми мои последние гроши,
Не отпускай меня вниз головою
В пространство мировое, шаровое!

1958 г.

Infant-Life

I am fond of living, afraid to die.
Under the voltage of the fisher's hand,
see how I thrash and strain like an ide,
reincarnating into word.

I am neither fish nor fisherman.
I'm a denizen of the soaked alcoves,
resemble Raskolnikoff,
bear my grievance like a violin.

Torture me—my face won't react.
Life is good, especially its final act—
whether in rain, nothing in my pocket,
or on Doomsday, a needle in my throat.

Ah, that dream! Infant-life, breathe.
You can take my last pennies,
but don't release me, head down,
into the world's spherical abyss.

1958

Голуби

Семь голубей – семь дней недели
Склевали корм и улетели,
На смену этим голубям
Другие прилетают к нам.

Живём, считаем по семёрке,
В последней стае только пять,
И наши старые задворки
На небо жалко променять:

Тут наши сизари воркуют,
По кругу ходят и жалкуют,
Асфальт крупитчатый клюют
И на поминках дождик пьют.

1958 г.

Pigeons

Seven days of the week—seven pigeons
devour our leftover crumbs
and wing away. Other pigeons
fly down, to replace them.

We live to count by seven—
but this final flock's only five.
Who would want heaven
in exchange for these old backyards?

Here, too, our gray ones coo,
waddle in circles, mourn, complain,
peck at the asphalt grains,
and at funerals, sip the rain.

1958

В дороге

Где чёрный ветер, как налётчик,
Поёт на языке блатном,
Проходит путевой обходчик,
Во всей степи один с огнём.

Над полосою отчужденья
Фонарь качается в руке,
Как два крыла из сновиденья
В средине ночи на реке.

И в жёлтом колыбельном свете
У мирозданья на краю
Я по единственной примете
Родную землю узнаю.

Есть в рельсах железнодорожных
Пророческий и смутный зов
Благословенных, невозможных,
Не спящих ночью городов.

И осторожно, как художник,
Следит проезжий за огнём,
Покуда железнодорожник
Не пропадёт в краю степном.

1959 г.

Passing By

Where black wind, like a robber,
sings a convict's slang,
a lone trackman walks, his fire
the only light on the plain.

In the zone of estrangement
a lantern swings at his side—
like wings from a dream
on a river in the waning night.

Here in the lullaby light
at the edge of the human,
by this singular feature
I recognize my native earth.

Through these iron rails, one hears
a hazy, prophetic call
of impossibly blessed
and sleepless cities at night.

And close as a painter
a train traveler tracks this light;
the railroad worker,
upon the vast steppe, slips from sight.

1959

Земное

Когда б на роду мне написано было
        Лежать в колыбели богов,
Меня бы небесная мамка вспоила
        Святым молоком облаков,

И стал бы я богом ручья или сада,
        Стерёг бы хлеба и гроба, –
Но я человек, мне бессмертья не надо:
        Страшна неземная судьба.

Спасибо, что губ не свела мне улыбка
        Над солью и жёлчью земной.
Ну что же, прощай, олимпийская скрипка,
        Не смейся, не пой надо мной.

1960 г.

Earthly

If it had been written in the stars
      that I would lie in the cradle of gods
and be raised by a heavenly wet-nurse
      on the holy milk of clouds,

I'd be the god of a stream or garden,
      guard some grain or grave.
But I don't want to be immortal. I'm human,
      and scared of an unearthly fate.

Thank God my lips have not been stitched
      into a grin, above the earth's salt
and bile. So long, Olympian violin,
      I don't want your laughter or song.

1960

Ветер

Душа моя затосковала ночью.

А я любил изорванную в клочья,
Исхлёстанную ветром темноту
И звёзды, брезжущие на лету
Над мокрыми сентябрьскими садами,
Как бабочки с незрячими глазами,
И на цыганской масленой реке
Шатучий мост, и женщину в платке,
Спадавшем с плеч над медленной водою,
И эти руки, как перед бедою.

И кажется, она была жива,
Жива, как прежде, но её слова
Из влажных «Л» теперь не означали
Ни счастья, ни желаний, ни печали,
И больше мысль не связывала их,
Как повелось на свете у живых.

Слова горели, как под ветром свечи,
И гасли, словно ей легло на плечи
Всё горе всех времен. Мы рядом шли,
Но этой горькой, как полынь, земли
Она уже стопами не касалась
И мне живою больше не казалась.

Когда-то имя было у неё.
Сентябрьский ветер и ко мне в жильё
Врывается –
              то лязгает замками,
То волосы мне трогает руками.

1960 г.

Wind

All night my soul roiled and pined.

Still, I loved the darkness torn apart
and lashed by gusts of wind.
I loved the stars' glimmering flight
like the blind eyes on butterflies
over wet September orchards,
the shaky bridge, the gypsy river,
and the woman above the slow water—
her kerchief flowing over her shoulder—
those hands, holding off disaster.

It was as if she were alive,
alive again, but her words'
liquid sounds now signified
neither joy nor sadness nor longing,
linked no longer by thinking—
unlike the syntax of the living.

Like a lit wick in wind, her voice flared
and guttered as if all human grief
bent her shoulders. We walked side by side,
her feet gliding like windswept leaves
along this earth, bitter as wormwood.
She was fading with every word.

Once upon a time she had a name.
September wind—even in my home—
bursts in—

         now clanging the hinges,
now caressing my hair with its fingers.

1960

Песня под пулями

Мы крепко связаны разладом,
Столетья нас не развели.
Я волхв, ты волк, мы где-то рядом
В текучем словаре земли.

Держась бок о бок, как слепые,
Руководимые судьбой,
В бессмертном словаре России
Мы оба смертники с тобой.

У русской песни есть обычай
По капле брать у крови в долг
И стать твоей ночной добычей.
На то и волхв, на то и волк.

Снег, как на бойне, пахнет сладко,
И ни звезды над степью нет.
Да и тебе, старик, свинчаткой
Ещё перешибут хребет.

1960 г.

Song Under the Bullet

We are so bound up in discord
centuries can't disentangle us—
I'm a warlock, you're a wolf. We're close
In the flowing dictionary of earth.

Shoulder to shoulder, like the blind
we're led along by destiny.
In the immortal dictionary of this country,
we're both condemned to die.

When we sing this Russian song
we trade our kindred blood, drop for drop,
and I become your night prey.
This is why we exist, wolf and warlock.

The snow smells sweet as a slaughterhouse
and not a single star shines above the steppe.
Old man, there's still time to get your face
and spine broken by a lead-tipped whip.

1960

К стихам

Стихи мои, птенцы, наследники,
Душеприказчики, истцы.
Молчальники и собеседники,
Смиренники и гордецы!

Я сам без роду и без племени
И чудом вырос из-под рук,
Едва меня лопата времени
Швырнула на гончарный круг.

Мне вытянули горло длинное,
И выкруглили душу мне,
И обозначили былинные
Цветы и листья на спине,

И я раздвинул жар берёзовый,
Как заповедал Даниил,
Благословил закал свой розовый,
И как пророк заговорил.

Скупой, охряной, неприкаянной
Я долго был землёй, а вы
Упали мне на грудь нечаянно
Из клювов птиц, из глаз травы.

1960 г.

To Poems

My poems: fledglings, heirs,
plaintiffs, and executors;
the silent ones, the loud,
the humble, and the proud.

As soon as the shovel of time
threw me onto the potter's wheel—
myself without kith or kin—
I grew beneath the hand, a miracle.

My neck was stretched
and my soul, hollowed wide,
and legends of flowers and leaves
serrated my ribs and spine.

I stoked the birch in the kiln
as Daniel commanded
and blessed my red temper
until I spoke as a prophet.

I had long been the earth—
ochre and arid, forlorn since birth—
but you fell on my chest by chance
from beaks of birds, from eyes of grass.

1960

Степь

Земля сама себя глотает
И, тычась в небо головой,
Провалы памяти латает
То человеком, то травой.

Трава – под конскою подковой,
Душа – в коробке костяной,
И только слово, только слово
В степи маячит под луной.

А степь лежит, как Ниневия,
И на курганах валуны
Спят, как цари сторожевые,
Опившись оловом луны.

Последним умирает слово.
Но небо движется, пока
Сверло воды проходит снова
Сквозь жёсткий щит материка.

Дохнёт репейника ресница,
Сверкнёт кузнечика седло,
Как радуга, степная птица
Расчешет сонное крыло.

И в сизом молоке по плечи
Из рая выйдет в степь Адам
И дар прямой разумной речи
Вернёт и птицам и камням,

The Steppe

The land swallows itself whole
and nuzzles the heavens,
patches up its memory's holes
with grasses and a man.

The grass is under horse's hoofs,
the soul in a box of bones,
and only the word, the word alone,
looms under the full moon.

Like Nineveh, the steppe stretches,
and boulders on burial mounds
drowse like ancient kings on watch,
drunk on lunar pewter.

Words will be the last to die.
But still the sky will move,
as long as water drills through
the hard sheet of earth.

A burdock eyelash will flutter,
the grasshopper's saddle, glimmer,
and a steppe bird will comb
its sleepy wing's rainbow.

In blue-grey milk up to his neck
Adam will walk from the garden
into the steppe and return
the gift of speech to birds and stones alike.

Любовный бред самосознанья
Вдохнёт, как душу, в корни трав,
Трепещущие их названья
Ещё во сне пересоздав.

1961 г.

The soul of souls, he'll breathe
a lover's fever of self-awareness
into the roots of grasses,
having remade their names in his sleep.

1961

Эвридика

У человека тело
Одно, как одиночка.
Душе осточертела
Сплошная оболочка
С ушами и глазами
Величиной в пятак
И кожей – шрам на шраме,
Надетой на костяк.

Летит сквозь роговицу
В небесную криницу,
На ледяную спицу,
На птичью колесницу
И слышит сквозь решётку
Живой тюрьмы своей
Лесов и нив трещотку,
Трубу семи морей.

Душе грешно без тела,
Как телу без сорочки, –
Ни помысла, ни дела,
Ни замысла, ни строчки.
Загадка без разгадки:
Кто возвратится вспять,
Сплясав на той площадке,
Где некому плясать?

И снится мне другая
Душа, в другой одежде:
Горит, перебегая
От робости к надежде,
Огнём, как спирт, без тени

Eurydice

Each person has only
one body, like a cell.
The soul is bone-weary
of this fated shell.
With ears and eyes
the size of a dime
and skin made of scars
stitched on a carcass.

It flies through the pupil
into the heavenly well,
onto the icy needle,
onto the bird's hearse.
It can hear, through bars
of its living jail,
the woods and fields rattle
the seven seas trumpet.

It's a shame for a soul
to be without the body's clothes,
with no intentions or designs,
no actions or lines.
Here's a riddle without the answer:
who will come again
having danced on these planks
when there's no one to dance?

I'm dreaming of another
soul in other clothes:
it burns, rushing like a spirit fire
from shyness to hope.
Shadowless, it walks

Уходит по земле,
На память гроздь сирени
Оставив на столе.

Дитя, беги, не сетуй
Над Эвридикой бедной
И палочкой по свету
Гони свой обруч медный,
Пока хоть в четверть слуха
В ответ на каждый шаг
И весело и сухо
Земля шумит в ушах.

1961 г.

into the distance, unseeable,
leaves the table
a cluster of lilacs.

Run along, child. Don't mourn
poor Eurydice.
Tap your copper hoop
with your stick, across the world—
as long as I hear one-fourth
of its noise, the earth
echoes the dry joy
of every plodding step.

1961

Первые свидания

Свиданий наших каждое мгновенье
Мы праздновали, как богоявленье,
Одни на целом свете. Ты была
Смелей и легче птичьего крыла,
По лестнице, как головокруженье,
Через ступень сбегала и вела
Сквозь влажную сирень в свои владенья
С той стороны зеркального стекла.

Когда настала ночь, была мне милость
Дарована, алтарные врата
Отворены, и в темноте светилась
И медленно клонилась нагота,
И, просыпаясь: «Будь благословенна!» –
Я говорил и знал, что дерзновенно
Моё благословенье: ты спала,
И тронуть веки синевой вселенной
К тебе сирень тянулась со стола,
И синевою тронутые веки
Спокойны были, и рука тепла.

А в хрустале пульсировали реки,
Дымились горы, брезжили моря,
И ты держала сферу на ладони
Хрустальную, и ты спала на троне,
И – Боже правый! – ты была моя.

Ты пробудилась и преобразила
Вседневный человеческий словарь,
И речь по горло полнозвучной силой
Наполнилась, и слово *ты* раскрыло
Свой новый смысл и означало *царь*.

First Times Together

Every second of our time together
we exulted, as if it were Epiphany,
we two alone in the world. Lighter
and braver than a bird's wing,
you skipped every other stair;
like dizziness, you led me
through wet lilacs, into your realm
on the other side of the mirror.

When night fell, I was given a gift.
The doors of the sanctuary opened:
in the darkness, nakedness was lit
and languidly bowed down.
And waking up, I said, *Blessed one,*
knowing that daring was my blessing.
When you slept, the lilacs
on the table reached down to touch your eyelids
with the blue universe.
Then those eyelids, touched by the azure,
were at peace, and your hand was warm.

While in the crystal sphere, rivers pulsed,
mountains smoked, seas dawned,
and in your palm you held
that crystal; your bed was a throne;
and—my God—you were mine.

Then you awakened, transfigured
the ordinary dictionary of man
until full-throated force filled
the neck of speech, and *thou* unveiled
its new meaning: *king of kings.*

На свете всё преобразилось, даже
Простые вещи – таз, кувшин, – когда
Стояла между нами, как на страже,
Слоистая и твёрдая вода.

Нас повело неведомо куда.
Пред нами расступались, как миражи,
Построенные чудом города,
Сама ложилась мята нам под ноги,
И птицам с нами было по дороге,
И рыбы подымались по реке,
И небо развернулось пред глазами...

Когда судьба по следу шла за нами,
Как сумасшедший с бритвою в руке.

1962 г.

Everything in the world was new again—
even plain things—this jug and that basin—
their layers of solid water
stood watch between us like a guard.

Something was leading us.
Built by miracle, whole cities split—
like mirages before our eyes.
And mint bowed beneath our feet,
and birds hovered above our heads,
and fish nosed against the river's flow,
and the sky unscrolled above the land...

while behind us, fate followed
like a madman with a razor in his hand.

1962

***

Мне опостылели слова, слова, слова,
Я больше не могу превозносить права
На речь разумную, когда всю ночь о крышу
В отрепьях, как вдова, колотится листва.
Оказывается, я просто плохо слышу
И неразборчива ночная речь вдовства.
Меж нами есть родство. Меж нами нет родства.
И если я твержу деревьям сумасшедшим,
Что у меня в росе по локоть рукава,
То, кроме стона, им уже ответить нечем.

1963–1968 гг.

[I've come to hate them, these words, words, words]

I've come to hate them, these words, words, words.
Why should I extol the right
to rational speech, when branches beat all night
against the roof like widows in ragged clothes?
For some reason, I can't seem to hear
the night language of widowhood, and it's hard
to read. Of course, there's a kinship between us.
Between us, no kinship. And even if I repeat
I'm in dew up to my elbows, to the crazy trees,
they only groan to answer me.

1963–1968

Поэт

Жил на свете рыцарь бедный...

Эту книгу мне когда-то
В коридоре Госиздата
Подарил один поэт;
Книга порвана, измята,
И в живых поэта нет.

Говорили, что в обличье
У поэта нечто птичье
И египетское есть;
Было нищее величье
И задёрганная честь.

Как боялся он пространства
Коридоров! Постоянства
Кредиторов! Он, как дар,
В диком приступе жеманства
Принимал свой гонорар.

Так елозит по экрану
С реверансами, как спьяну,
Старый клоун в котелке
И, как трезвый, прячет рану
Под жилеткой из пике.

Оперённый рифмой парной,
Кончен подвиг календарный, –
Добрый путь тебе, прощай!
Здравствуй, праздник гонорарный,
Чёрный белый каравай!

The Poet (Osip Mandelstam)

Once there lived a poor knight…
—Alexander Pushkin

A life ago, in a dark room
at the State House of Publishing,
A poet gave me this volume.
The spine's now cracked,
the author, no longer living.

They say he looked
like an ancient bird
that once flew over Egypt.
They saw his beggared
greatness, his taut honor.

Yet he feared the expanse
of corridors, the constancy
of creditors. Like a gift, he
accepted his award
in a fit of affected glee.

Just like the old clown
who crawls across the movie screen
in chapeau and bow, as if stoned,
and, as if sober, hides the wound
beneath his vest, beneath his overcoat.

Feathered by couplets, his feat
over the calendar is complete.
Farewell. May all your roads
be smooth. Greetings, paid
holiday, black and white loaf

Гнутым словом забавлялся,
Птичьим клювом улыбался,
Встречных с лёту брал в зажим,
Одиночества боялся
И стихи читал чужим.

Так и надо жить поэту.
Я и сам сную по свету,
Одиночества боюсь,
В сотый раз за книгу эту
В одиночестве берусь.

Там в стихах пейзажей мало,
Только бестолочь вокзала
И театра кутерьма,
Только люди как попало,
Рынок, очередь, тюрьма.

Жизнь, должно быть, наболтала,
Наплела судьба сама.

1963 г.

of a book. He curved words,
smiled with his beak,
locked arms with anyone,
feared being alone,
read poems to strangers.

That's how a poet should be.
I roam the globe,
afraid of being alone.
For the hundredth time, lonely,
I read his book again.

So few landscapes in his poems—
only the confusion of train stations,
a theater's commotion,
only faces seen at random,
the marketplace, a queue, prison.

Life babbled and blabbed to him—
his fate was transcription.

1963

Явь и речь

Как зрение – сетчатке, голос – горлу,
Число – рассудку, ранний трепет – сердцу,
Я клятву дал вернуть моё искусство
Его животворящему началу.

Я гнул его, как лук, я тетивой
Душил его – и клятвой пренебрёг.

Не я словарь по слову составлял,
А он меня творил из красной глины;
Не я пять чувств, как пятерню Фома,
Вложил в зияющую рану мира.
А рана мира облегла меня;
И жизнь жива помимо нашей воли.

Зачем учил я посох прямизне,
Лук – кривизне и птицу – птичьей роще?
Две кисти рук, вы на одной струне,
О явь и речь, зрачки расширьте мне,
И причастите вашей царской мощи,

И дайте мне остаться в стороне
Свидетелем свободного полёта
Воздвигнутого чудом корабля,
О два крыла, две лопасти оплота,
Надёжного, как воздух и земля!

1965 г.

Reality and Speech

As sight gives to retina, voice to throat,
number to reason, early thrill to the heart,
I gave an oath to return
the life-giving source to my art.

Then bending art like a bow, strangling
the bowstring, I ignored my vow.

I did not compile the lexicon; word by word
it created me out of red clay. Not I
who placed the five senses, like the fingers
of Thomas, into the gaping wound of the world.
The wound of the world enfolded me
and now life is, despite our desires.

Why did I try to teach straightness to the staff,
curvature to the branch, nesting to the bird?
Two palms—wrapped around a single string—
O reality and speech, widen my pupils,
commune your kingly power.

Let me stand aside
and witness the flight
of a ship built by miracle.
O two wings, two buoying blades
reliable as air and earth.

1965

Рукопись

А. А. Ахматовой

Я кончил книгу и поставил точку
И рукопись перечитать не мог.
Судьба моя сгорела между строк,
Пока душа меняла оболочку.

Так блудный сын срывает с плеч сорочку,
Так соль морей и пыль земных дорог
Благословляет и клянёт пророк,
На ангелов ходивший в одиночку.

Я тот, кто жил во времена мои,
Но не был мной. Я младший из семьи
Людей и птиц, я пел со всеми вместе

И не покину пиршества живых –
Прямой гербовник их семейной чести,
Прямой словарь их связей корневых.

1960 г.

Manuscript

To Anna Akhmatova

I finished the book, affixed the last period
and could not look at it again.
Between the lines my fate was burned
while my soul sloughed off its skin.

This is how the prodigal son tears off his robes,
this is how the prophet curses and blesses
the salt of the seas, the dust of mortal roads
and challenges the angel to wrestle.

I was a person who lived in this age,
but wasn't me. I sang with everyone.
From the family of people and birds, I was the least—

simple genealogist of their lineage,
primal etymologist of rooted communion.
I won't give up the earthly feast.

1960

III.

Gather My Wax When
Morning Arrives

1965–1977

Жизнь, жизнь

I.

Предчувствиям не верю и примет
Я не боюсь. Ни клеветы, ни яда
Я не бегу. На свете смерти нет.
Бессмертны все. Бессмертно всё. Не надо
Бояться смерти ни в семнадцать лет,
Ни в семьдесят. Есть только явь и свет,
Ни тьмы, ни смерти нет на этом свете.
Мы все уже на берегу морском,
И я из тех, кто выбирает сети,
Когда идёт бессмертье косяком.

II.

Живите в доме – и не рухнет дом.
Я вызову любое из столетий,
Войду в него и дом построю в нём.
Вот почему со мною ваши дети
И жёны ваши за одним столом, –
А стол один и прадеду и внуку:
Грядущее свершается сейчас,
И если я приподымаю руку,
Все пять лучей останутся у вас.
Я каждый день минувшего, как крепью,
Ключицами своими подпирал,
Измерил время землемерной цепью
И сквозь него прошёл, как сквозь Урал.

Life, Life

I.

I don't believe in omens, nor fear
foreboding signs. No poisons or lies
will strike me down. There is no death on earth;
everyone's immortal. Nothing will die.
There's no need to fear the end—at seventeen
or seventy. There's only this life, this light
on earth; there's no darkness or death.
We're all already on the seashore,
and I'm one of those who hauls in the nets
when immortality swims past a shoal.

II.

If you live in a house, the house will not fall.
Summon any of the centuries,
I'll enter and build a house in it.
That is why they are with me,
our beloveds and children, around my table
large enough for ancestors and grandchildren:
the future turns its face to us now,
and if I raise my hand a little,
all five rays will dwell among you.
Every day I used my collarbones
as if they were logs to shore up the past—
I measured time with cubits and spans
then crossed its mountain range.

III.

Я век себе по росту подбирал.
Мы шли на юг, держали пыль над степью;
Бурьян чадил; кузнечик баловал,
Подковы трогал усом, и пророчил,
И гибелью грозил мне, как монах.
Судьбу свою к седлу я приторочил;
Я и сейчас, в грядущих временах,
Как мальчик, привстаю на стременах.

Мне моего бессмертия довольно,
Чтоб кровь моя из века в век текла.
За верный угол ровного тепла
Я жизнью заплатил бы своевольно,
Когда б её летучая игла
Меня, как нить, по свету не вела.

1965 г.

III.

I tailored the age to fit my frame,
then we headed south, made the steppe dust fly.
Tall weeds fumed. A grasshopper played;
touching its antenna to a horseshoe, it prophesied;
like a monk, it threatened me with destruction.
I strapped my fate to the saddle.
And even now, in the time to come,
I stand up in stirrups like a boy.

My immortality suits me well—
my blood flows from age to age.
I would have paid with my life, whimsically,
for a warm and sturdy corner—
if the flying needle had not tugged me
like a thread across the universe.

1965

Ночь под первое июня

Пока ещё последние колена
Последних соловьёв не отгремели
И смутно брезжит у твоей постели
Боярышника розовая пена,

Пока ложится железнодорожный
Мост, как самоубийца, под колёса
И жизнь моя над чёрной рябью плёса
Летит стремглав дорогой непреложной,

Спи, как на сцене, на своей поляне,
Спи, эта ночь твоей любви короче, –
Спи в сказке для детей, в ячейке ночи,
Без имени в лесу воспоминаний.

Так вот когда я стал самим собою,
И что ни день – мне новый день дороже,
Но что ни ночь – пристрастнее и строже
Мой суд нетерпеливый над судьбою...

1965 г.

The Night Before the First of June

And while the last notes of the last
loud nightingales continue to glide,
and the pink foam of hawthorn
gleams like dawn at your bedside,

while the train bridge lies down
under the wheels, a suicide,
and my life flies headlong
above the river's black rippled bed—

sleep, as if on stage, in your glade.
This night is briefer than your love.
Sleep in this fairy tale, in this night
hive, in memory's woods.

Now I've become whom I was meant
to be. With each new day, each day is dearer.
With every night, my judgment of fate
grows even more skewed, severe.

1965

***

О, только бы привстать, опомниться, очнуться
И в самый трудный час благословить труды,
Вспоившие луга, вскормившие сады,
В последний раз глотнуть из выгнутого блюдца
Листа ворсистого
хрустальный мозг воды.

Дай каплю мне одну, моя трава земная,
Дай клятву мне взамен – принять в наследство речь,
Гортанью разрастись и крови не беречь,
Не помнить обо мне и, мой словарь ломая,
Свой пересохший рот моим огнём обжечь.

1965 г.

[O, if only I could rise, regain memory and consciousness]

O, if only I could rise, regain memory and consciousness,
and at the most difficult hour, bless the labor
that reared the meadows and nurtured the orchards,
and one last time, swallow the crystal brain of water
from the concaved sheet
                    of a downy leaf.

Give me one drop, my mortal grass,
an oath to inherit speech,
to grow a larynx, not sparing blood,
to forget myself, and tearing up my words,
burn your parched mouth with my fire.

1965

***

Я по каменной книге учу вневременный язык,
Меж двумя жерновами плыву, как зерно в камневерти,
И уже я по горло в двухмерную плоскость проник,
Мне хребет размололо на мельнице жизни и смерти.
Что мне делать, о посох Исайи, с твоей прямизной?
Тоньше волоса плёнка без времени, верха и низа.
А в пустыне народ на камнях собирался, и в зной
Кожу мне холодила рогожная царская риза.

1966 г.

[By the book of stone I learn a tongue outside of time]

By the book of stone I learn a tongue outside of time,
between two millstones I swirl like a grain,
have already entered the two-dimensional plane.
The windmill of life, of death, has ground down my spine.

What should I do, O staff of Isaiah, with your straightness?
This timeless veil is thinner than hair and boundless.
The people in the desert would gather and rest on the stones;
even in the heat, the matted kingly chasuble would chill me to
    the bone.

1966

***

Вот и лето прошло,
Словно и не бывало.
На пригреве тепло.
Только этого мало.

Всё, что сбыться могло,
Мне, как лист пятипалый,
Прямо в руки легло,
Только этого мало.

Понапрасну ни зло,
Ни добро не пропало,
Всё горело светло,
Только этого мало.

Жизнь брала под крыло,
Берегла и спасала,
Мне и вправду везло.
Только этого мало.

Листьев не обожгло,
Веток не обломало...
День промыт, как стекло,
Только этого мало.

1967 г.

[And now summer has left]

And now summer has left
as if it never came at all.
It's warm still where the sun falls.
But it's not enough.

Whatever I wanted to happen
fell right into my hands
like a five-fingered leaf.
But it's not enough.

The just and unjust
played their necessary part
and burned into light.
But it's not enough.

Life tucked me behind its back
and shielded me from cuffs.
I've had such good luck.
But it's not enough.

My leaves have yet to blaze;
my branches have not yet broken.
The day is clear as glass—
but it's not enough.

1967

***

И я ниоткуда
Пришёл расколоть
Единое чудо
На душу и плоть,

Державу природы
Я должен рассечь
На песню и воды,
На сушу и речь.

И, хлеба земного
Отведав, прийти
В свечении слова
К началу пути.

Я сын твой, отрада
Твоя, Авраам,
И жертвы не надо
Моим временам,

А сколько мне в чаше
Обид и труда...
И после сладчайшей
Из чаш –
            никуда?

1967 г.

[From nowhere at all]

From nowhere at all
I arrived to split
the indivisible miracle
into flesh and blood.

I have to dismember
the kingdom of nature
into song and water,
into land and word,

and tasting the salt
of earth, to arrive in
the glow of language,
where my path begins.

I am your son,
your joy, Abraham;
though this age demands
no victims,

my cup is full
with grievances, with labor.
After the sweetest of meals
—then
            where?

1967

***

Стихи попадают в печать,
И в точках, расставленных с толком,
Себя невозможно признать
Бессонниц моих кривотолкам.

И это не книга моя,
А в дальней дороге без вёсел
Идёт по стремнине ладья,
Что сам я у пристани бросил.

И нет ей опоры верней,
Чем дружбы неведомой плечи.
Минувшее ваше, как свечи,
До встречи погашено в ней.

1967 г.

[Their commas exact and sensible]

Their commas exact and sensible,
poems slip into publication—
but my insomniac monologue
doesn't see itself inside that spine.

It's not really my book—
it's floating without oars
into the far rapids, some boat
I'd left untied at the pier.

It rides on the shoulders
of unfamiliar but faithful friends.
Let it carry their past
like snuffed candles—until we meet again.

1967

Памяти А. А. Ахматовой

I.

Стелил я нежную постель,
Луга и рощи обезглавил,
К твоим ногам прильнуть заставил
Сладчайший лавр, горчайший хмель.

Но марта не сменил апрель
На страже росписей и правил.
Я памятник тебе поставил
На самой слёзной из земель.

Под небом северным стою
Пред белой, бледной, непокорной
Твоею высотою горной

И сам себя не узнаю,
Один, один в рубахе чёрной
В твоём грядущем, как в раю.

Август 1968 г.

To the Memory of A. A. Akhmatova

I.

I beheaded groves and meadows
to make a tender bed.
Bitter hops and sweet laurel
would cling to your feet.

March did not relieve April
to guard our order, our laws.
So I built you a memorial
on this soil rich in tears.

Under the northern sky I stand
before your white, rebellious
Parnassian height,

and cannot recognize who I am,
alone in the black shirt
in your future, as in paradise.

August, 1968

II.

Когда у Николы Морского
Лежала в цветах нищета,
Смиренное чуждое слово
Светилось темно и сурово
На воске державного рта.

Но смысл его был непонятен,
А если понять – не сберечь,
И был он, как небыль, невнятен
И разве что – в трепете пятен
Вокруг оплывающих свеч.

И тень бездомовной гордыни
По чёрному Невскому льду,
По снежной Балтийской пустыне
И по Адриатике синей
Летела у всех на виду.

Апрель 1967 г.

II.

When misery lay covered in flowers
in the Cathedral of St. Nicholas,
a word both humble and stark
gleamed its austere dark
on the wax of sovereign lips.

But its meaning was beyond us,
and if we'd understood, we wouldn't remember.
It was opaque as fiction—
and if it could be revealed , it could,
but only in the quiver of dripping tapers.

And over the black Neva ice,
over the snowy desert Baltic,
and over the blue Adriatic,
the shadow of your homeless pride
flew before our gaze.

April, 1967

III.

Домой, домой, домой,
Под сосны в Комарове...
О, смертный ангел мой
С венками в изголовье,
В косынке кружевной,
С крылами наготове!

Как для деревьев снег,
Так для земли не бремя
Открытый твой ковчег,
Плывущий перед всеми
В твой двадцать первый век,
Из времени во время.

Последний луч несла
Зима над головою,
Как первый взмах крыла
Из-под карельской хвои,
И звёзды ночь зажгла
Над снежной синевою.

И мы тебе всю ночь
Бессмертье обещали,
Просили нам помочь
Покинуть дом печали,
Всю ночь, всю ночь, всю ночь.
И снова ночь в начале.

Апрель 1967 г.

III.

Homeward, homeward, homeward,
under the pines of Komarovo.
O, my mortal angel
in lacy three-cornered scarf
with wreaths above your head,
your wings ready to unfurl.

Just as snow in trees
burdens not the branches,
your open ark's no burden
for earth, hovering above our gaze,
beyond your twenty-first century,
from your age to the ages.

Winter flung one last spire
of light above its head,
like the first wingflutter
of Karelian pine,
and above the snowy blue,
stars prickled the sky.

All night we promised
you immortality, all night
we longed for you
to take us from the house of grief—
all night, all night, all night,
as it was in the beginning.

April, 1967

IV.

Пó льду, пó снегу, по жасмину,
На ладони, снега бледней,
Унесла в свою домовину
Половину души, половину
Лучшей песни, спетой о ней.

Похвалам земным не доверясь,
Довершив земной полукруг,
Полупризнанная, как ересь,
Через полог морозный, через
Вихри света –

                смотрит на юг.

Что же видят незримые взоры
Недоверчивых светлых глаз?
Раздвигающиеся створы
Вёрст и зим иль костёр, который
Заключает в объятия нас?

3 января 1967 г.

IV.

Over ice and white, over jasmine,
in her palm paler than snow,
she took to her coffin
half a soul, half a song
in praise of her.

Not trusting eulogy,
finishing her earthly half-circle,
half-recognized like heresy,
through the icy curtain, through
the vortices of light—
                                    she looks south.

What does the invisible gaze
of her clear, distrustful eyes see?
The parting gates, opening to miles
and winters, or the great fire
come to engulf us?

January 3, 1967

V.

И эту тень я проводил в дорогу
Последнюю – к последнему порогу,
И два крыла у тени за спиной,
Как два луча, померкли понемногу.

И год прошёл по кругу стороной.
Зима трубит из просеки лесной.
Нестройным звоном отвечает рогу
Карельских сосен морок слюдяной.

Что, если память вне земных условий
Бессильна день восстановить в ночи?
Что, если тень, покинув землю, в слове
Не пьёт бессмертья?
                            Сердце, замолчи,
Не лги, глотни ещё немного крови,
Благослови рассветные лучи.

12 января 1967 г.

V.

I saw this shade off, on her last
trip, to the final threshold,
and two wings behind the shade's back,
like two rays, slowly faded.

How did the earth orbit, once again?
Winter trumpets from the forest clearing,
and mica ghosts of Karelian pines
reply to its horn by clanging.

What if, outside the earthly, memory
can't, at night, remake a day?
What if, after leaving earth, the shade
can't drink immortality in words?
                          Enough, heart.
Don't lie. Swallow a little more blood
and bless the dawn's shards of light.

January 12, 1967

***

Мамка птичья и стрекозья,
Помутнела синева,
Душным воздухом предгрозья
Дышит жухлая трава.

По деревне ходит Каин,
Стёкла бьет и на расчёт,
Как работника хозяин,
Брата младшего зовёт.

Духоту сшибает холод,
По пшенице пляшет град.
Видно, мир и вправду молод,
Авель вправду виноват.

Я гляжу из-под ладони
На тебя, судьба моя,
Не готовый к обороне,
Будто в Книге Бытия.

1967 г.

[Wet-nurse of dragonflies and birds]

Wet-nurse of dragonflies and birds,
the blue sky is dim,
the withered grass inhales the swelter
as if before a storm.

In the village Cain shatters
window after window, calls his brother
to the final account
as a master would a servant.

The cold batters the air.
Hail dances on the wheat.
It's true, really, the world
is young, and Abel is to blame.

With my open palm I shade
my face, my fate—
unready, defenseless
as in the book of Genesis.

1967

После войны

I.

Как дерево поверх лесной травы
Распластывает листьев пятерню
И, опираясь о кустарник, вкось,
И вширь, и вверх распространяет ветви,
Я вытянулся понемногу. Мышцы
Набухли у меня, и раздалась
Грудная клетка. Лёгкие мои
Наполнил до мельчайших альвеол
Колючий спирт из голубого кубка,
И сердце взяло кровь из жил, и жилам
Вернуло кровь, и снова взяло кровь,
И было это как преображенье
Простого счастья и простого горя
В прелюдию и фугу для органа.

After the War

I.

Like a tree in forest underbrush
spreads out its leafy hands
and, leaning on a shrub, propagates
its branches sideways, widthwise—
so I shot up, adagio. My muscles
swelled, my rib cage expanded,
my lungs filling with the prickly wine
of a sky-blue chalice, down
to the alveoli, and my heart
borrowed blood from the veins and
returned it and took the blood again,
and it was like a transfiguration
of simple happiness and plain grief
in a prelude and fugue for organ.

II.

Меня хватило бы на всё живое –
И на растения, и на людей,
В то время умиравших где-то рядом
И где-то на другом конце земли
В страданиях немыслимых, как Марсий,
С которого содрали кожу. Я бы
Ничуть не стал, отдав им жизнь, бедней
Ни жизнью, ни самим собой, ни кровью.
Но сам я стал как Марсий. Долго жил
Среди живых, и сам я стал как Марсий.

II.

I would suffice for all living things,
both plants and people,
who'd died somewhere near
and at world's end
in unimaginable suffering, like Marsyas,
flayed alive. If I'd given them my life,
I would not have become any poorer
in life, in myself, in my blood.
But I became like Marsyas. Having lived long
among the living, I became like Marsyas.

III.

Бывает, в летнюю жару лежишь
И смотришь в небо, и горячий воздух
Качается, как люлька, над тобой,
И вдруг находишь странный угол чувств:
Есть в этой люльке щель, и сквозь неё
Проходит холод запредельный, будто
Какая-то иголка ледяная...

III.

Sometimes, when you lie in the summer heat
and look at the sky, and the hot air
rocks like a cradle above you, you
find a strange angle of senses:
there is a flaw in the crib, and through it
an outer cold descends, as if
an icy needle...

IV.

Как дерево с подмытого обрыва,
Разбрызгивая землю над собой,
Обрушивается корнями вверх,
И быстрина перебирает ветви,
Так мой двойник по быстрине иной
Из будущего в прошлое уходит.
Вослед себе я с высоты смотрю
И за́ сердце хватаюсь. Кто мне дал
Трепещущие ветви, мощный ствол
И слабые, беспомощные корни?
Тлетворна смерть, но жизнь ещё тлетворней,
И необуздан жизни произвол.
Уходишь, Лазарь? Что же, уходи!
Ещё горит полнеба за спиною.
Нет больше связи меж тобой и мною.
Спи, жизнелюбец! Руки на груди
Сложи и спи!

IV.

Like a tree splashing the earth
above itself, having collapsed from a steep
undermined by water, roots in the air,
the rapids plucking its branches—
so my double on the other rapids
travels from future to past.
From another height, I trail myself
with my eyes, clutch my chest. Who gave me
trembling branches, a sturdy trunk
yet weak, helpless roots?
Death is vile, but life is worse,
and there's no binding its tyranny.
Are you leaving, Lazarus? Well, go away!
Behind you, half the sky still blazes.
Nothing holds us together. Sleep,
vivacious one, fold your hands
on your chest and sleep.

V.

Приди, возьми, мне ничего не надо,
Люблю – отдам и не люблю – отдам.
Я заменить хочу тебя, но если
Я говорю, что перейду в тебя,
Не верь мне, бедное дитя, я лгу...
          О, эти руки с пальцами, как лозы,
          Открытые и влажные глаза,
          И раковины маленьких ушей,
          Как блюдца, полные любовной песни,
          И крылья, ветром выгнутые круто...
Не верь мне, бедное дитя, я лгу,
Я буду порываться, как казнимый,
Но не могу я через отчужденье
Переступить, и не могу твоим
Крылом плеснуть, и не могу мизинцем
Твоим коснуться глаз твоих, глазами
Твоими посмотреть. Ты во сто крат
Сильней меня, ты – песня о себе,
А я – наместник дерева и Бога,
И осуждён твоим судом за песню.

1969 г.

V.

Come by, take this, I don't need anything,
what I love I give away, and what I don't
I'll give away. I want to replace you,
but if I say that I'm going to turn into you,
don't believe me, poor child, I'm lying.
> O, these hands with fingers like vines,
> these open and wet eyes,
> these shells of small ears
> like saucers filling with a love song,
> and wings curved sharply by wind.
Don't believe me, poor child, I lie.
I try to break away like one condemned,
but I cannot cross through
this strangeness, can't wave your wings
or touch your lids, or see through
your eyes. A hundred times
stronger than me, you sing
about your self. I'm deputy of the tree
and God, and by your judgment
sentenced for my song.

1969

***

Река Сугаклея уходит в камыш,
Бумажный кораблик плывёт по реке.
Ребёнок стоит на песке золотом,
В руках его яблоко и стрекоза.
Покрытое сеткой прозрачной крыло
Звенит, и бумажный корабль на волнах
Качается, ветер в песке шелестит,
И всё навсегда остается таким...

А где стрекоза? Улетела. А где
Кораблик? Уплыл. Где река? Утекла.

1933–1969 гг.

[The Sugakleya disappears into the reeds]

The Sugakleya disappears into the reeds,
a paper boat treads the river.
A child lingers on the golden sand,
an apple and a dragonfly in his hand.
Veiled by a rainbow net, the wings
hum, the boat plunges into the waves,
wind rustles the sand, and everything
stays this way forever.

Where is that dragonfly? Flew away.
That boat? Sailed off. That river? Flowed away.

1933–1969

***

И это снилось мне, и это снится мне,
И это мне ещё когда-нибудь приснится,
И повторится всё, и всё довоплотится,
И вам приснится всё, что видел я во сне.

Там, в стороне от нас, от мира в стороне
Волна идёт вослед волне о берег биться,
А на волне звезда, и человек, и птица,
И явь, и сны, и смерть – волна вослед волне.

Не надо мне числа: я был, и есмь, и буду,
Жизнь – чудо из чудес, и на колени чуду
Один, как сирота, я сам себя кладу,
Один, среди зеркал – в ограде отражений
Морей и городов, лучащихся в чаду.
И мать в слезах берёт ребёнка на колени.

1974 г.

[I dreamed all this, and this I'm dreaming]

I dreamed all this, and this I'm dreaming
and I'll dream this again. Everything
will repeat and realize its final form,
and you will dream whatever I dream.

Beyond us, beyond the world, a wave
beats against the far shore.
On that wave man rides, and bird, and star,
reality and dreams, and death, wave after wave.

I have no need of ciphers:
I was, am, will be. Life itself is wonder.
Alone, I seat myself upon its lap, like an orphan.
Alone, among mirrors, I'm fenced in by reflections
of seas and cities shining in dark fumes.
Mother, weeping, will pull this child into her arms.

1974

Мартовский снег

По такому белому снегу
Белый ангел альфу-омегу
Мог бы крыльями написать
И лебяжью смертную негу
Ниспослать мне как благодать.

Но и в этом снежном застое
Еле слышно о непокое
Сосны чёрные говорят:
Накипает под их корою
Сумасшедший слёзный разлад.

Верхней ветви – семь вёрст до неба,
Нищей птице – ни крошки хлеба,
Сердцу – будто игла насквозь:
Велика ли его потреба, –
Лишь бы небо впору пришлось.

А по тем снегам из-за лога
Наплывает гулом тревога,
И чужда себе, предо мной
Жизнь земная, моя дорога
Бредит под своей сединой.

1974 г.

Snow in March

In a snow this white
a white angel could alight
and with its wings, write
Alpha to Omega, make the death-cry
of a swan sound like grace.

But in this impasse
the black pines mutter
about their lack of peace—
a mad lacrimal disorder
seethes beneath their crust.

Will the highest bough ever reach
beyond itself, the poor bird eat
ever again? The heart is pierced,
always, with a needle thought—
how to fit the sky.

Across this snow, from the ravine
a droning worry fills my ears.
My life on earth, my path
estranged from itself, is raving
under its white hair.

1974

***

Ещё в ушах стоит и гром и звон:
У, как трезвонил вагоновожатый!

Туда ходил трамвай, и там была
Неспешная и мелкая река –
Вся в камыше и ряске.
                    Я и Валя
Сидим верхом на пушках у ворот
В Казённый сад, где двухсотлетний дуб,
Мороженщики, будка с лимонадом
И в синей раковине музыканты.

Июнь сияет над Казённым садом.

Труба бубнит, бьют в барабан, и флейта
Свистит, но слышно, как из-под подушки:
В полбарабана, в полтрубы, в полфлейты
И в четверть сна, в одну восьмую жизни.

Мы оба
            (в летних шляпах на резинке,
В сандалиях, в матросках с якорями)
Ещё не знаем, кто из нас в живых
Останется, кого из нас убьют,
О судьбах наших нет ещё и речи,
Нас дома ждёт парное молоко,
И бабочки садятся нам на плечи,
И ласточки летают высоко.

1976 г.

[That thunder still rings in the ears]

That thunder still rings in the ears:
how loud the conductor's bell

where a streetcar passed, and here
an unhurried, shallow river,
its reeds and duckweed.
          Valya and I
ride horseback on cannons at the gate
to the public orchard, near a historic oak,
ice cream vendors, a booth with lemonade,
and musicians in a blue shell.

June shines over the orchard.

Trumpets mutter, drums thrum, and a flute
whistles, muffled as if from under a pillow:
half the drums, half the trumpets, half the flute.
At a quarter dream, at an eighth a life,

neither of us
          (in elastic-banded summer hats,
sailor's jackets with anchors, and sandals)
knows yet of the days to come—
who will survive, and who will be killed.
Our fates remain opaque as fresh milk
awaiting us at home, nearby.
On our shoulders, butterflies rest,
and swallows fly high in the sky.

1976

***

А все-таки я не истец,
Меня и на земле кормили:
– Налей ему прокисших щец,
Остатки на помойку вылей.

Всему свой срок и свой конец,
А всё-таки меня любили:
Одна: – Прощай! – и под венец,
Другая крепко спит в могиле,

А третья у чужих сердец
По малой капле слёз и смеха
Берёт и складывает эхо,
И я должник, а не истец.

1977 г.

[I'm no plaintiff, I will not sue]

I'm no plaintiff, I will not sue.
I've received my share of meat
—*spoon for him that spoiled soup,*
chuck the rest on the garbage heap.

Everything has its term and its end.
I testify that I've been loved.
One woman said farewell and left
for the altar. Another sleeps in her grave.

The third gathers tears
and laughter from strangers,
so laughter and tears would echo.
No, I'm no plaintiff. I'm a debtor.

1977

***

Просыпается тело,
Напрягается слух.
Ночь дошла до предела,
Крикнул третий петух.

Сел старик на кровати,
Заскрипела кровать.
Было так при Пилате,
Что теперь вспоминать?

И какая досада
Сердце точит с утра?
И на что это надо –
Горевать за Петра?

Кто всего мне дороже,
Всех желаннее мне?
В эту ночь – от кого же
Я отрёкся во сне?

Крик идёт петушиный
В первой утренней мгле
Через горы-долины
По широкой земле.

1976 г.

[From its dark sleep the body wakes]

From its dark sleep the body wakes
and the ear strains to hear.
The night has died into day.
The third cock has crowed.

An old man sits on the bed
and the bed groans beneath him
as it has since Pilate's time.
Why should it be any different?

What is this shame that knives
inside the heart?
And why must one grieve,
even now, for Peter?

Whom do I cherish most in this life,
who's most beloved to me?
And this night, who have I
denied knowing as I slept?

In the pre-dawn haze
the cock's cry travels
across valleys and hills
and will not rest for the rest of our days.

1976

Жили-были

Вся Россия голодала,
Чуть жила на холоду,
Граммофоны, одеяла,
Стулья, шапки, что попало
На пшено и соль меняла
В девятнадцатом году.

Брата старшего убили,
И отец уже ослеп,
Всё имущество спустили,
Жили, как в пустой могиле,
Жили-были, воду пили
И пекли крапивный хлеб.

Мать согнулась, постарела,
Поседела в сорок лет
И на худенькое тело
Рвань по-нищенски надела;
Ляжет спать – я то и дело:
Дышит мама или нет?

Гости что-то стали редки
В девятнадцатом году.
Сердобольные соседки
Тоже, будто птицы в клетке
На своей засохшей ветке,
Жили у себя в аду.

Но картошки гниловатой
Нам соседка принесла
И сказала:
            – Как богато

Once Upon a Time

All Russia was starving,
freezing, barely living.
Gramophones, quilts, hats,
tables—whatever we had
we traded for salt and grain
in the year 1919.

My older brother killed,
my father gone blind—
everything we owned we sold.
We lived, once upon a time,
as if in a grave, drank no tea
and made bread from weeds.

My mother was forty
but stooped over and gray.
She dressed her slender frame
in rags that fit a beggar.
At night in bed, I'd wonder:
is Mama still breathing?

Guests were rare
in that benighted year.
Compassionate neighbors
like birds behind bars
on branches, in their cells,
lived in their own hells.

One day a neighbor gave us
a gift of rotten potatoes.
She said: *Even the beggars
once lived like tsars.*

Жили нищие когда-то.
Бог Россию виноватой
Счёл за Гришкины дела.

Вечер был. Сказала:
                    – Ешьте! –
Подала лепёшки мать.
Муза в розовой одежде,
Не являвшаяся прежде,
Вдруг предстала мне в надежде
Не давать ночами спать.

Первое стихотворенье
Сочинял я, как в бреду:
«Из картошки в воскресенье
Мама испекла печенье!»
Так познал я вдохновенье
В девятнадцатом году.

1977 г.

This is God's retribution
for Rasputin's sin.

It was evening, and calling us close,
Mother served the potatoes:
                              Now eat!
The muse, in rose-colored clothes,
whose shape I had not known,
now came to me, hoping
to keep me from sleep.

I composed my first poem
as if in a delirium:
          Only my mother could bake
          a potato made of cake—
this is all it took
to be inspired
that benighted year.

1977

***

Меркнет зрение – сила моя,
Два незримых алмазных копья;
Глохнет слух, полный давнего грома
И дыхания отчего дома;
Жёстких мышц ослабели узлы,
Как на пашне седые волы;
И не светятся больше ночами
Два крыла у меня за плечами.

Я свеча, я сгорел на пиру.
Соберите мой воск поутру,
И подскажет вам эта страница,
Как вам плакать и чем вам гордиться,
Как веселья последнюю треть
Раздарить и легко умереть,
И под сенью случайного крова
Загореться посмертно, как слово.

1977 г.

[My sight, which was my power, now blurs]

My sight, which was my power, now blurs—
two invisible diamond spears;
my hearing subsides, full of ancient thunder
and the breathing of my father's house.
These knots of thick muscles slacken
like grey oxen lying upon the ploughed field;
the wings behind my shoulders yield
no light when evening darkens.

I am a candle. I burned at the feast.
Gather my wax when morning arrives
so that this page will remind you
how to be proud and how to weep,
how to give away the last third
of happiness, and how to die with ease—
and beneath a temporary roof
to burn posthumously, like a word.

1977

Afterword

Erotic Soyuz: 25 Propositions on Translating
(Arseny Tarkovsky)

Philip Metres

1.

Every essay on (the impossibility of) translation resembles every other, but this one is happy in its own way. Like a striptease that leads only to more clothing, let's begin with a contradiction: generalities are never interesting. The particular is the place of all the juice and joy, all the scald and sin. For example, what's an adequate translation for форточка (*fortochka*)—that little window that opens in a bigger window that does not open?

2.

Another generality masquerading as a particular: language is limestone, porous enough to let the world in and out again, always changed by the water's flow. If poetry is in fact "what is lost in translation," it is because our own words often fail to describe, inscribe, transcribe, or circumscribe our lives. The failures of translation, then, are not failures between languages as much as a property of language itself.

3.

Yet, the translator believes that different languages have enough open edges, even contact zones, like the human body, that they can near or even touch each other. The closer the worlds of those languages (for example, Romance languages or Slavic languages or Finno-Ugric languages), the more edges will fit (almost seamlessly) with other edges. What the translator sees is how many edges have no partner. When I first spent time in Russia, I was amazed how people used the term "на улице" to signify "outside." Literally, the term means "on the street." Another term that Russians use is "на дворе," which means "in the [court] yard." There are many words for outside—снаружи, or exterior—but people don't use it in quite the same way. Inscribed in our languages are slightly different conceptualizations of space. That's why I began the poem "Ashberries," about the time I spent living in Russia: "Outside, in a country with no word for outside,/they cluster on trees, red bunches." Of course this country has a word for outside—it has many words for outside—but what I was gesturing toward was the gap between languages, the gap between different conceptions of space.

4.

Language dictionaries suggest otherwise, but the very fact that words have deep roots makes exact one-to-one word translation difficult, one step more difficult than seeking synonyms in Roget's Thesaurus. If you've done this before, you know exactly what I'm talking about. Have a word, then try to find an adequate synonym. Each possibility feels slightly off, like glasses with the wrong prescription. And each synonym for synonym leads you further and further from anything that approximates seeing. Every word, every word worth its salt, carries with it a kind of irreducible particularity—its primal sounds, its weight in the mouth, its richly layered conscious and unconscious connotations and associations, both public and private. Words are like people, only older and more idiosyncratic.

5.

During the fall of the Soviet Union, Russians often had to import English words to describe the new (economic) system that suddenly infiltrated their lives, words for "fun," "know-how," "businessman," "discount," "sale," etc. And, of course, the Russians have a whole bag of words associated with Soviet, peasant, and other cultural formations distant from our American experience: how to find a single term for колхоз ("kolkhoz," or "collective farm") or кулак ("kulak," meaning both "landowning peasant" and "fist") that would carry at least some of the connotations of those words? Or, more mundanely, how to find an American English word to describe the acidic reaction one gets from biting into something sour? The Russians have a single word for that: оскомина.

6.

The particular at hand, what we wish to touch, what we wish to touch us, is the work of Russian poet Arseny Tarkovsky, with which I've been wrestling (in tag-team with Dimitri Psurtsev) for the past five years. Tarkovsky, a lifelong poet and translator, the father of the great filmmaker Andrei Tarkovsky, knew himself all too well the miseries of translation, as he wrote in his poem "Translator":

> For what did I spend
> My best years on foreign words?
> O, Eastern translations,
> How you hurt my head.

Actually, of course, he wrote nothing of the kind. He wrote:

> Для чего я лучшие годы
> Продал за чужие слова?
> Ах, восточные переводы,
> Как болит от вас голова.

Or as an email once encoded it:

> ??????????????????????????????
> ??????????????????????????????
> ??????????????????????????????
> ??????????????????????????????

Somehow, this seems to be a most adequate representation of the poetics of translation.

7.

How can we get close to Tarkovsky? First, there is the fact of Russian poetry's acute and irreducible particularities, the most acute and irreducible its relationship to meter. The regularity of Russian conjugations and declensions, the flexibility of word order in sentence meaning, and the multisyllabic nature of Russian words all combine to create a seemingly endless wellspring of rhymes and metrical possibilities. In contrast to the poetries of the West, which inhaled modernism's breath of free verse and only rarely return to the formal rooms of strict meters, Russian poetry has, until only very recently, been almost entirely faithful to its highly organized and lush meters. In Tarkovsky's poetry alone, one can find poems not only in iambic, but also in trochaic, dactylic, anapestic, amphibrachic, not to mention folksong prosodic patterns, unrhymed metrical poems, and, yes, even free verse. It's as if, in the United States, our poetry, metrically speaking, plays its tune within the limits of the pop form, while in Russia, whole symphonies continue to be produced.

8.

But that metaphor suggests a low culture/high culture distinction that distracts from the persistence of complex meters (and rhyme) in Russian poetry. During the 20th century, when Anglo-American poetry confronted the brave new world of modernism and mass culture, free verse articulated a response to new conditions of production and reception, both to attempt to "make it new" and also resist the new advertising cooptation of the poetic "jingle." In the early Soviet period, poets innovated mightily—from Velemir Khlebnikov's заумь (*zaum'*) sound poems to Vladimir Mayakovsky's new brutalism in the 1910s and 1920s. But as Socialist Realism began to dominate, and many great poets faced repression, the great mnemonic capabilities of Russian poetry served, literally, to allow unpublished poems to persist, in the minds of their readers. The story of Nadezhda Mandelstam's memorizing her husband Osip's poems, detailed in *Hope Against Hope*, is but one stunning example of how Russian poetry's aural commitments (and the Russian people's commitments to poetry) enabled a kind of secret history of the soul to continue.

9.

Even if the Russian literary tradition does delve deep into the darkness and misery and mystery of human existence, the music of Russian poetry is so undeniable, so playful, so often ecstatic, and has persisted for so long, it suggests the secret pleasures of a people who have been seen in the West as the stern patrons of unhappiness ("every unhappy family," etc.). It is, indeed, what makes translating Russian poetry most difficult, and why readers of Russian poetry in translation—say, the English poetry version of Anna Akhmatova or Osip Mandelstam—mainly receive a picture of a grim and absurd reality but not much of a sense of what it sounds like when a pure music collides with the grim or the absurd.

10.

Perhaps the translator is a traitor to the native. It's not for nothing that translators are said to use "native informants" to gather intelligence on these strange and dangerous poems. Translators, at times, are literal and figurative colonizers, threatening to domesticate or erase the other in the name of "cultural understanding" or "universal human values." When American translators brought Russian literature into English during the Cold War, it was often summoned to serve a specific political function—not to bring cultural understanding, but to bring down the Soviet Union. And when the Soviet Union fell, the government money that had poured into Slavic Departments and presses disappeared overnight.

11.

Of course, what brought me to study Russian poetry may indeed have been Ronald Reagan, who in the 1980s referred to the Soviet Union as the "evil empire." I was immediately intrigued, believing that no people is evil. When I shared this story with poet Sergey Gandlevsky, he said, "you know, when I heard Reagan say that, I thought he was right."

12.

And equally, that the translator can be traitor to her own people, the way the peacebuilder or a lyric poet can seem a traitor to the tribe. In the words of Charles Simic: "Here is something we can all count on. Sooner or later our tribe always comes to ask us to agree to murder.... The lyric poet is almost by definition a traitor to his own people. He is the stranger who speaks the harsh truth that only individual lives are unique and therefore sacred. He may be loved by his people, but his example is also the one to be warned against." The translator lingers in contested territory, where sectarianism compels us/them, ours/theirs. The translator is the one who reminds us that difference is not demonic, but daemonic. The translator, possessed by voices and visions that s/he can only dimly understand, cannot not speak in this forked (and forked-over) tongue.

13.

Back to Tarkovsky. Tarkovsky's deft and diverse deployment of various meters and rhyme schemes presents an almost insurmountable translation problem: how to demonstrate his near-polyphonic facility for variable patterns of rhythm and sound over the course of many poems, without flattening that work to a dull iambic or free verse style with some half-hearted gesture toward off-rhyme? Dimitri Psurtsev and I considered various, sometimes radical, options. One option, briefly considered: if, in American poetry, the "normative" mode is intonational free verse, then why not make all the "normative" Russian poems with rhyme and meter into that intonational free verse, and all the experimental (free verse or unrhymed poems) into poems with meter and rhyme?

14.

Another, more rigidly systematic option would be simply to translate all the dactylic poems as dactylic poems, the iambics as iambic, and so on. This, frankly, seemed more possible but also literalist, since a poem in dactylic in Russian will mean something different than it will in American poetry. We decided against this rigid and misplaced conservatism, encouraged by the notion of the "semantic aura of meter." Kirill Taranovski (and later Mikhail Gasparov) argues that each meter in Russian poetry carries with it the themes and associations of previous poets' employment of those meters; the very idea that a poem's meters are embedded in a larger discourse of form complicates any simplistic application of meter from poetic tradition to poetic tradition.

15.

Our resolution of this interminable impasse between Russian metric and American poetry has been at once less systematic and more organic. Since Tarkovsky's poetry is driven by its music, propelled by rhythm and rhyme, then our translation should make every reasonable attempt to make a similar music. For example, in his war-era portrait, "Ехал из Брянска в теплушке слепой..." ("A blind man was riding an unheated train"), Tarkovsky employs a dactylic trimeter (plus a final beat) in couplets that echo Nikolay Nekrasov's jaunty folk song meters, recreating Nekrasov's dissonant effect with the grim picture of a blind man traveling in the provinces in a cargo train during the Nazi invasion. I began to find the translation in amphibrachs, a peculiar three-part beat of unstressed-stressed-unstressed. The translation begins:

A blind man was riding an unheated train,
From Bryansk he was traveling home with his fate.

Fate whispered to him so the whole car could hear:
and why should you worry over blindness and war?

It's good, she was saying, you're sightless and poor.
If you were not blind, you'd never survive.

Without rhythm and rhyme, we would risk turning Tarkovsky into a standard Socialist Realist for our reader (even though original Socialist Realists in Russian culture do use meters and rhyme)—losing precisely what makes him a great poet. But we tread carefully, knowing how meter and rhyme also risk turning him into Mother Goose.

16.

For a free verse poem like such as "Град на Первой Мещанской" ("Hail on First Petit-Bourgeois Street," published in *Asymptote*), we opted to remove all punctuation and create greater disjunction on the level of the line (even though normative punctuation exists in the original), in order to reproduce the astonishing effect of free verse to the Russian ear. Perhaps even this does not quite go as far as recreating the unusual feeling of a Russian reader encountering the opening of the poem:

tongues in the tower
pound the bells to sound
wind lifts   everyone
rushes into entrances   doors
slam   along the sidewalk
sandals patter   rain chasing
her heart   pounds
her wet dress itches
& the roses are soaked

17.

Translating metrical richness, however, is not the only problem in translating Tarkovsky. The music of words—from the problem of rhyme to inner alliteration—also presents issues. For example, the war poem "Иванова Ива" (published in *Asymptote*) relies on the musical play in Russian between "iva" (willow) and the soldier's name "Ivan."

Иванова ива

Иван до войны проходил у ручья,
Где выросла ива неведомо чья.

Не знали, зачем на ручей налегла,
А это Иванова ива была.

В своей плащ-палатке, убитый в бою,
Иван возвратился под иву свою.

Иванова ива,
Иванова ива,
Как белая лодка, плывет по ручью.

To think: inside the name of the tree is the name of the man. The man inside the tree—as if anticipating the coffin, enclosed inside the wood. Ideally, one might translate this poem as "Will's Willow," which suggests the shared destiny of soldier and the tree of mourning—but such a choice could confuse readers about the place of the poem. We opted for "Valya"—the name of the poet's brother who was killed in the Civil War—which contains the "l" and vaguely echoes the "w" with the "v." Here's our translation, in its entirety:

Valya's Willow

Before the war Valya walked along the creek,
where a willow grew for who knows who.

Though why it stood on the creek, no one knew.
Valya owned that willow.

Killed in action, Valya came back
under his willow in his military cloak.

Valya's willow,
Valya's willow,
like a white boat floating on the creek.

18.

Finally, there is the problem of translating Tarkovsky's own
world—both his cultural-historical context and his own
personal vision. In "К Стихам" ("To Poems"), Tarkovsky's
characteristic quasi-Christian pantheism explores the origins
of his poetry, addressing his own poems as if they were his
children. It ends:

I had long been the earth—
ochre and arid, forlorn since birth—
but you fell on my chest by chance
from beaks of birds, from eyes of grass.

These final lines presented a confusion that thankfully was
clarified by the late poet and translator F.D. Reeve, who noted
that the "eyes of grass" is a reference to how fields of grasses
would contain wildflowers, whose "eyes" would seed the earth.
In what is an all too typical problem in translation, what
appeared to be pure abyssal surrealism—"eyes of grass"—was
an associative leap from one place to another place, very much
on (and in!) earth. How stunning that a poet of such great humil-
ity (from *humus*, earth) is able to pull off speaking as earth.

19.

Or this poem, "Бабочка в госпитальном саду" ("Butterfly in
the Hospital Orchard"), about Tarkovsky's days on the edge

between life and death after his gangrenous leg required multiple amputations. The lightness and beauty of the meter and rhyme, as if following the motions of the butterfly, hovers just outside all catching it. The word play at the end of the second stanza of the poem relates to the fact that the word for butterfly, "бабочка," has only two vowels—"a" and "o." It's as if this creature, at its center, produces only the vowels of awe: A! O! The English vowels "u" and "y"—which we first tried— seemed more like a matrix of existential questioning. It lacks the utter wonder of the Russian, which is why we returned to it in the end.

Each of the poems, then, presents its own challenges—metrical, sonic, and etymological. To register the uniqueness of Tarkovsky's style, and his range as a poet, has become the ultimate challenge. We want to bring you to a vivid reflection of his vision and music, and in this bilingual edition, allow you to peer over to the other, original, Cyrillic shore.

20.

It turns out that failure—the dominant metaphor in so much talk about translation—is not the right metaphor at all. How's this? Translation as erotic/asymptotic—about nearing, longing, stretching one's language toward what it might become. The original as sacred text toward which we long. If poetry is, as Allen Grossman has proposed, an Orphic attempt to reach the Beloved, then the translator is nothing if not Orpheus, at every moment longing to turn and be sure that the beloved still follows. Only a complete turn back will cause the beloved to fade forever. I'm reminded, suddenly, of the moment I learned that in polite written Russian, the addressed "you" is always capitalized, and the word "I" is not.

21.

Or this: translation as transformation. Translation as a co-creative, procreative act. Two languages come together and make a third thing. Robert Lowell's notorious *Imitations*, treat the original texts not as an impossibly-distant object of idealization, but a source of inspiration and invitation, something to meet and make love with. Fady Joudah recently said that he wished his translations of Palestinian poet Mahmoud Darwish are not in English, but "Arabish." May these Tarkovsky poems be "Russianish."

22.

Translations are beautiful monsters. If all translators are Frankenstein, the main question then becomes: is the creature alive? Those grab bags of other organs and skin, stolen from the graveyards of other traditions whose sensibilities are not always our own, grafted into something that approximates a whole. Has the translator provided the lightning rod, gathered the electricity? Monstrous beauty, do you breathe?

23.

Since the 1960s, the Russians have flown a series of spacecraft called Союз. Soyuz. We have heard it pronounced "Soy-use," emphasis on the "soy." *I am*, but only in Spanish. In Russian, it sounds like "sigh-use," the emphasis on "use." It means "union." To think: all these Unions flying about the sky, hovering above and around our planet, in space.

24.

These Unions, in fact, have something called *translation thrusters*. Translation, in physics, describes the "motion of a body in which every point of the body moves parallel to and the same distance from every other point of the [other] body."

25.

In the end, translators believe in the possibility of translation, as poets must believe in the impossibility of translation—even as they engage in that impossible process with every poem, even in their native tongue. But difference does not lead, necessarily, to irreconciliability. So this: that the two language-poems work on their relation, to find those points parallel, the edges that hold against other edges—providing a fit that each will wear, and will wear each, in its own way.

Notes

Candle
According to Marina Tarkovskaya (daughter of the poet), a number of Tarkovsky's poems through the years were written in memory of Maria Gustavovna Faltz, his first love, who died in 1932. In addition to "Candle," other Faltz-related poems in this volume include: "The table is set for six," "Wind," "Eurydice," and "First Times Together."

Ignatievo Forest
The poem reflects the difficult relationship with Tarkovsky's first wife, Maria Ivanovna Vishnyakova (1907–1979), mother of Andrey (1932) and Marina (1934), whom he left in 1937.

The table is set for six
Tarkovsky read the poem to friends in the early spring 1941, in the presence of Marina Tsvetayeva (1892–1941) who was in love with the poet. Her poetic reply, "I'm still repeating the first line," turned out to be her last poem. In it, Tsvetayeva reproaches Tarkovsky for not inviting her to this "gathering of six," including Tarkovsky, his dead father and brother, his first love, and Grief and Loss. The first two stanzas of Tsvetaeva's poem are as follows:

> I'm still repeating the first line
> And the well-worn refrain:
> — "The table was set for six" —
> But you forgot the seventh one.

The six of you unhappy.
Your faces sparkling like rain...
How could you for such a table
Forget the seventh one.

Yesterday morning I began waiting for you
This poem read by Tarkovsky was used in the iconic film *Mirror* (1974) by his son, Andrey Tarkovsky. It was highly unusual for a young poet at that period of Soviet history to write so simply and directly about private love, when Soviet Realism pressured writers to focus on "the problems of the people" or "collective labor," etc.

Chistopol Notebook
This poetic sequence was written in Chistopol, Tartarstan, which had become a shelter for the Soviet Writers Union, which was evacuated from Moscow during the Second World War. It concerns both the ongoing war and Tarkovsky's grief and guilt over the suicide of Marina Tsvetaeva, a friend of the poet, who hung herself in Yelabuga, on the Kama River. The sequence includes sonnets, folk-inspired verse, and one patriotic poem. Poem "V." alludes to Tarkovsky's work unloading firewood in October and November. The final poem of the sequence might refer to the fact that the Marina's gravesite remains unknown.

Beautiful Day
This poem was likely written on the Front. The poem's Russian title literally means "White Day," the poet's unique way of rendering the idea of purity and bliss of the past that can be relived only through memory. Characteristically, the line "Bely-bely den'"—literally, "a very white day"—was the original title of the film *Mirror* at its scriptwriting stage. The mirror image and title of the film may have also come from Arseny's poetry (since "First Times Together" is also featured there).

A blind man was riding an unheated train

The poem was written in a cargo train between Bryansk and Zhivodovka. The line "Let me just raise your eyelids wide open" is an allusion to Viy, the all-seeing demon of Ukrainian folk tales that Gogol popularized in his story "Viy." The demon's eyelids drooped to the floor, and required its minions to lift them in order to see. His command was "Raise my eyelids."

A German machinegunner will shoot me in the road, or

During the initial stage of the Second World War, Russian "valenki" boots, as well as regular highboots, were in short supply during the long winter, and boots of the dead were sometimes stripped by individual soldiers or special squads whose mission was to recover the boots for soldiers who had none. In one gruesome story, the frozen legs of hundreds of corpses were actually sawed off by Russian troops because they could not remove the critically-needed boots, which were frozen on.

Butterfly in the Hospital Orchard

The vowels in the Russian word for butterfly are "a" and "o"— vowels filled with awe and woe. In the "bandit" post-Soviet 1990's, a Russian bank used the line "Flying from shadow into the light," with an image of butterfly, as an ad slogan on posters and billboards, hinting at money-laundering—which angered Tarkovsky fans.

Valya's Willow

In Russian, the poem moves almost purely by sound, as "Ivanova Iva" means "Ivan's Willow."

Saturday, June 21st, 1941

The date of Germany's surprise attack on the Soviet Union, which brought them into the Second World War, was early morning of June 22nd, 1941. The final line references how people would glue two broad lines of paper in a diagonal cross on glass windows so that the glass would be preserved from the shock-wave of bombs and heavy artillery fire.

Field Hospital

As noted in the introduction, this poem deals with Tarkovsky's war injury and near-death experience from gangrene. His second wife, Antonina, rescued him from the terrible field hospital to Moscow. In January 1944, he had yet another operation (a larger amputation, following several previous amputations on his left leg) which finally stopped the gangrene.

Things

Tarkovsky's litany of objects that evoke the pre-Soviet world include: the "Lightning Lamp" (a kerosene lamp with a broad wick and narrowed glass top); the black powder of gunpowder; stylish turn-of-the-century tipped mustaches; Semyon Nadson, the decadent poet who died of consumption, known for his characteristic use of three-syllable meters; bared shoulders and hat ostrich feathers of aristocratic women (also referenced in Alexander Blok's famous "The Unknown Woman"); "tall futurists," a reference to Vladimir Mayakovsky and his yellow jacket; and finally, three pre-Revolutionary alphabet Cyrillic letters he mentions (see original) that we chose not to name in the translation. Four letters were abolished during the Bolshevik spelling reform in order to simplify spelling for the masses.

You evening light, gray

In her review of the first Tarkovsky book, Anna Akhmatova wrote "To those who still don't have the book I recommend they get their hands on a copy somehow, to give it a most rigorous review. This book isn't afraid of anything. Is it possible to have a more elegant line than: '...the stitch of your clothes / made of wind and rain'?"

From the Window
This poem alludes to Vladislav Khodassevich's "Ballad," in which "someone hands me [the poet] a heavy lyre through the window."

Song Under the Bullet
The image of a wolf echoes Osip Mandelstam's famous line: "The wolf-age pounces on my shoulders." Tarkovsky's "patriotic" title has little to do with the meaning of the poem and, according to Marina Tarkovskaya, was part of his attempt to ease it into publication.

The Steppe
The ancient city of Nineveh, alluded to in the *Book of Jonah* as an "exceeding great city," that lay on the eastern bank of the Tigris in modern-day Mosul, Iraq.

Wind
Reviewing the first book of Tarkovsky, Akhmatova wrote that this poem "seems to me one of the summits of contemporary Russian poetry."

First Times Together
Tarkovsky's reading of this poem occurs at a pivotal moment in his son's much-lauded film *Mirror*.

The Poet (Osip Mandelstam)
The poem is an elegy for Osip Mandelstam, whom Tarkovsky knew in the 1920s and 1930s before Mandelstam's arrest and deportation to Siberia. Tarkovsky compares Mandelstam to Charlie Chaplin (whom Mandelstam alluded to in a number of his poems), whose *Circus* is implied by the fourth stanza.

And now summer has left
This poem recited by Stalker in Andrey Tarkovsky's influential film, the postapocalyptic *Stalker*.

To the Memory of A. A. Akhmatova
On March 9, 1966, Tarkovsky accompanied Akhmatova's coffin from Moscow to Leningrad; she was buried in Komarovo, a village where Akhmatova summered in a small dacha she named "Budka," meaning "sentry box" and also "kennel." Tarkovsky read the fourth part of the poem at her graveside. The "great fire / come to engulf us" alludes to the fire that friends made at the burial. According to one account: "The only thing I remember clearly, we tried to make a fire, because she liked fires."

That thunder still rings in the ears
This poem references the poet's brother, Valya (Valera), who was killed in the Russian Civil War. In Russian, the poem is unrhymed until the final stanza.

Once Upon a Time
This poem details the period of chaos and starvation during the Soviet Revolution and Civil War in 1919. It employs a ballad meter, and evokes the fairy tale tradition by beginning with the Russian equivalent of "once upon a time."

About the translators

Philip Metres is the author and translator of a number of books and chapbooks including *Sand Opera* (Alice James Books, 2015), *Compleat Catalogue of Comedic Novelties: Poetic Texts of Lev Rubinstein* (Ugly Duckling Presse, 2014), *A Concordance of Leaves* (Diode Press, 2013), *abu ghraib arias* (Flying Guillotine Press, 2011), *To See the Earth* (Cleveland State University Poetry Center, 2008), and *Behind the Lines: War Resistance Poetry on the American Homefront Since 1941* (University of Iowa Press, 2007). His work has garnered two NEA fellowships, the Thomas J. Watson Fellowship, five Ohio Arts Council Grants, the Beatrice Hawley Award, two Arab American Book Awards, the Cleveland Arts Prize, the Anne Halley Prize, the PEN/Heim Translation grant, a Russian Institute for Literary Translation grant, and the Creative Workforce Fellowship. He is a professor of English at John Carroll University in Cleveland.

Dimitri Psurtsev, a Russian poet and translator of British and American authors, is a professor at Moscow State Linguistic University and lives outside Moscow with his wife Natalia and daughter Anna. His two books of poetry, *Ex Roma Tertia* and *Tengiz Notepad*, were published in 2001 by Yelena Pakhomova Press and translations of his poems were published by the *Hudson Review* in 2009 and 2011. In 2014 Dimitri received, along with Philip Metres, a PEN/Heim Translation Fund grant for *I Burned at the Feast: Selected Poems of Arseny Tarkovsky*.

About the author

Arseny Alexandrovich Tarkovsky was born in the Ukrainian city of Elisavetgrad (now Kirovohrad) in 1907 and moved to Moscow in 1923, working as a newspaper journalist and publishing his first poems. By the late 1930s, he had become a noted translator of Turkmen, Georgian, Armenian, Arabic, and other Asian poets. During the Second World War, he served as a war correspondent for the Soviet Army publication Battle Alarm from 1942 to 1944, receiving the Order of the Red Star for valor. His first book of poems was suppressed by the authorities in 1946, prior to publication. Tarkovsky's first volume of his own poems, *Before the Snow*, emerged in 1962, when the poet was 55, and rapidly sold out. His fame widened when his son, the internationally-acclaimed filmmaker Andrei Tarkovsky, included some of his father's poems in his films. He died in 1989, just before the Soviet Union fell.